THE TRUMPING OF AMERICAN POLITICS

The Trumping of American Politics

The Strange Case of the 2016 Presidential Election

Michael A. Genovese

CAMBRIA
PRESS

Amherst, New York

Photos on front cover: Trump by Marc Nozell, Clinton and
Sanders by Voice of America, Kasich by Office of Ohio Governor
John R. Kasich, Rubio by US Senate, and Cruz by Frank Fey.

Library of Congress Cataloging-in-Publication Data

Names: Genovese, Michael A., author.

Title: The trumping of American politics :
the strange case of the 2016 presidential election /
by Michael A. Genovese, President,
World Policy Institute at Loyola Marymount University.

Description: Amherst, New York : Cambria Press, [2017] |
Includes bibliographical references and index.

Identifiers: LCCN 2017017844 |

ISBN 9781604979855 (alk. paper)

Subjects: LCSH: Presidents--United States--Election--2016. | Trump,
Donald, 1946- | United States--Politics and government--2009-2017.

Classification: LCC JK526 2016 G46 2017 |
DDC 324.973/0932--dc23
LC record available at https://lccn.loc.gov/2017017844

To Gaby,
who will guide me through the Trump years

TABLE OF CONTENTS

LIST OF TABLES

LIST OF FIGURES

ACKNOWLEDGEMENTS

Producing a book is a team sport. I was fortunate to have a great team on my side. At the Global Policy Institute, Ashley Oshiro, Sabrina Leung, Breanne Schneider, John Pickhaver, Héctor Blanes Pomares, Dani Jordan, Jeremy Seland, Ogonwa Nwankwo, and Elizabeth Garza were dedicated, hardworking, and always congenial. And a big shout-out to Kevin Wallsten at California State University, Long Beach, whose election data and charts I included in this book. At Cambria Press, Toni Tan and David Armstrong were consummate professionals and supportive teammates. And at home, my smoking-hot wife Gaby was, as always, the most amazing woman I've ever met. To you all, my deepest thanks.

THE TRUMPING OF
AMERICAN POLITICS

CHAPTER 1

INTRODUCTION

This is the story of America's controversial 2016 presidential election. It was as entertaining as it was bizarre, as shocking as it was unusual. If nothing else, Donald Trump put the *fun* back into dysfunctional.

Back in my Vietnam War protest days, there was a chant that marchers would often repeat in unison: "The whole world is watching; the whole world in watching." In 2016, the whole world was watching as Donald Trump won the Republican nomination for president on the strength of bigotry, sexism, populist insurgency, and economic fears. He was the face of America to the world. And he is now our president.

And yet, one is left with the hope that we are so much better than that. "Make America Great Again?" No, we are a great, if imperfect, country, a shining city on the hill, even as we grope and fumble our way forward; a country that is best when we honor our ideals, but one that when we falter, we really falter. Our ideals distinguish us as our humanity keeps reminding us that we should be humble. It is when we strive for those ideals, when we reach out and up, that we are at our best. Sadly, this book is not the story of America at its best, but it is a reminder that we must be vigilant in the face of bigotry, loving in response to hatred, compassionate in the face of selfishness, and true to that which is best in us, in response to efforts that would have us behave otherwise.

American presidential elections tend to be long, costly, and superficial. And the 2016 race fulfilled that trifecta very well. It took nearly three long, often-tedious years to select Donald Trump as the 45th President of the United States. In the United Kingdom it takes about six weeks. Overall, the 2016 national elections cost billions of dollars. The race also tended towards the ridiculous as swaggering bombast trumped (no pun intended) thoughtful policy discussions, and the pompous outmaneuvered the ponderous. The Trump media magnet pulled everyone into its wake, and serious public policy discussion was relegated to the back pages of our sadly disappearing daily newspapers.

Ours is a top-leadership selection process difficult to defend and harder still to explain (especially to non-Americans). I often travel to teach and lecture in Europe and am often asked to explain the American presidential selection system to people who simply cannot fathom how the most powerful nation on earth elects the most important leader on earth with such a bizarre and broken system. The Electoral College? No other nation has such a baroque electoral mechanism, and others wonder how the globe's chief proponent of democracy could employ such an odd, undemocratic device for selecting its president—one in which the candidate with the most votes could lose the election, as was the case for Al Gore in the 2000[1] and again for Hillary Clinton in 2016. And money! How, they often ask, could the country that goes to war to impose democracy on other nations, allow big money and corporations to "buy" its presidents? Our presidential selection system simply does not make sense to outsiders. Should it make sense to us?

Does the process attract and reward the best potential candidates, or does it repel good potential candidates from running in the first place? Does the process by which we elect presidents reward the worst of the candidates, and punish the best? And does it properly test the skills and temperament of potential presidents? Is what it takes to get elected different from what it takes to govern effectively? Does this system fulfill our democratic promise? Is this the best we can do?

In elections, we not only pick our leaders, we also have a national discussion on our collective future. We (the people) are supposed to tell them (elected officials) where we want the nation to be headed. We give the directions. Or do we?

A functional electoral system should:

1) produce several talented people who seek the office

2) test the qualities necessary to govern effectively

3) expose those qualities of character or temperament that a president should not have

4) be fair and transparent

5) present to the voters issues of substance

6) offer a clear choice regarding directions in which to take the nation.

As presently structured, our top-leadership selection does a poor job in virtually all of these categories. It has evolved over time as a patchwork of reforms, evolution, and devolutions. It is not a coherent, systematic process. In the conclusion, we will briefly explore several ways to create a better selection process.

James M. Burns called our leadership selection process the "least functional" in the world. And Adlai Stevenson II—who ran for and lost the office on two occasions (both times to Dwight D. Eisenhower)—once said that "anyone who could be elected president, didn't deserve the office." He also told the story of a woman supporter at a campaign rally who shouted out "Mr. Stevenson, all thinking people support you," to which Stevenson replied, "That's wonderful, but I need a majority." The great lawyer Clarence Darrow noted that "When I was a boy, my mother told me that in America, anyone could be president—and now, looking at the two candidates, I'm inclined to believe her!" Why does hardly anyone say a good word about our presidential selection system? Is it really that broken?[2]

Every four years it is our job to hire a president. What do we look for, and what *should* we look for in a president? In hiring a president or hiring any top executive, we would want skill, experience, a proven track record of success, positive endorsements from other people who know the candidate and give honest evaluations, and someone who has values close to ours (or the organizations). If we were to put together a want ad for a new president it would read something like this:

> WANTED: A chief executive of a large multidimensional organization that is directly responsible for more than 320 million people. The successful applicant should have substantial executive/managerial experience, be of the highest character, have a proven track-record of success, must be able to work well with others and be able to bargain, compromise, and build coalitions and consensus. The occupant of this job will have very limited power to accomplish the very high expectations placed upon him/her. Long hours (12-hour days will be the norm for entire time in office). Must be very dignified as job entails numerous ceremonial duties. Should have experience in the following fields: national security, economics, health care, crisis management, education, immigration, fighting terrorism, diplomacy, environmental management, building a democracy, working with an independent and very powerful Board of Directors (we call them Congress), wide experience in public speaking.

Some background in the military would be helpful but not necessary. Must be a high energy, thick-skinned person who can take constant criticism as he/she and their family live in a 24/7 fishbowl with virtually no privacy. Performance evaluations occur every day, often several times each day, and are circulated across the globe. Any blemish on one's record will be blown out of proportion. Must also have a winning personality, exhibit strength and resolve where necessary, but be able to compromise most of the time. Be willing to order thousands of your employees to their possible death, and be willing to kill an undetermined number of our organizations competitors. Should be a people person. The applicant will have to get elected by an angry and demanding electorate, roughly half of whom will hate him/her from day one. Entry fee to apply is over $1 billion. Poor people, middle-class workers, and those unable or unwilling to raise this money should not apply. Note: The job interview will take three years, and you will hardly be able to see your family for those three years. If the applicant, and/or the applicant's spouse, family, and associates have any "skeletons" in their closet, these will be exposed on national media. Working environment is generally pleasant enough, but the pay is not commensurate with what one might expect. A good deal of travel (in high style) will be required. Housing is included, along with round-the-clock assistance to attend to the successful applicant's every need.

So why would any sane person even seek the job? Some seek it for the wrong reasons—to wield power, to feel important. Others seek the job for the right reasons: to do good things for the country. Being president, as difficult and frustrating as it is, can give one the opportunity to do important things to improve the lives of citizens.

The saga of the 2016 presidential election reads like a bad made-for-television movie. It had everything: sex (and a lot of it), intrigue (from the Russians), conflict (to say the least), big lies (and little ones), violence (to the nation's sense of self), big money (of the billion-dollar variety), and a whole lot of surprises. It was Donald and Hillary's excellent adventure, and I invite you to come along for the ride—but buckle your seat belts, it's a pretty rough ride.

Notes

1. Howard Gillman, *The Votes that Counted: How the Court Decided the 2000 Presidential Election* (Chicago: University of Chicago Press, 2003); and Jeffrey Tobin, *Too Close to Call: The Thirty-Six-Day Battle to Decide the 2000 Election* (New York: Random House Trade Paperbacks, 2002).
2. Nelson W. Polsby and Aaron Wildavsky, *Presidential Elections: Strategies and Structures of American Politics* (New York: Rowman & Littlefield Publishers, 2011).

CHAPTER 2

THE PRIMARIES

Words like *unusual, unprecedented, crazy, strange,* and *unbelievable* all accurately describe the 2016 presidential race. Actually, they may even understate what went down.

First of all, the race was decided even before it got started. Jeb Bush for the Republicans and Hillary Clinton for the Democrats were prohibitive favorites going into the race, awaiting only the official coronation instead of a campaign. It was a slam dunk. Then The Donald came on the scene. And so did Bernie Sanders.

For Hillary Clinton, it was déjà vu. In 2008 she entered the contest as the favorite, but a little-known freshman senator named Barack Hussein Obama came out of nowhere and took the nomination and the presidency from her hands. It couldn't happen again, could it?

This time around there did not seem to be any serious rivals, but that is what the Clinton camp has mistakenly believed eight years earlier.

For Jeb, (and he decided to campaign merely as Jeb, apparently hoping to distance himself from his brother), the road seemed a bit more crowded but no more difficult.

By January 1, 2015, it looked like "The Jeb and Hillary Show." For Clinton, a Joe Biden run might be a problem, but the tragic death of his son on March 30, 2015, understandably took the fire out of Biden. Beyond that, the Democrat's bench was very thin. A few non-threatening candidates—Jim Webb, former Senator from Virginia; Lincoln Chafee, former governor of Rhode Island; Martin O'Malley, former Maryland governor; and Bernie Sanders, an Independent Senator (not even a Democrat) from Vermont, the self-proclaimed Democratic Socialist. It was a group of nonstarters, and Clinton probably felt safe.

But Clinton had baggage: Bill, her controversial ex-president husband, ongoing questions about her e-mails while serving as secretary of state, the baggage of Benghazi, millions of dollars in speaking fees from Wall Street groups, and "Clinton fatigue" all proved to be death by a thousand cuts. Moreover, Clinton's campaign seemed flat and lifeless. There was no driving message, no passion, and no "reason" to support her.

And then Sanders exploded on the scene. This 74-year-old leftist of Jewish descent took the world by storm. 2016 was another angry voter election, and Sanders captured the mood of the angry voters in the Democratic Party. What were Democrats angry about? The 1%, income inequality, Wall Street. Economic fears turned to anger, then to passion, and Sanders was their voice.

For Jeb, he had the money, the support of the establishment (which worked both ways for him), and an air of inevitability that might chase challengers away.

And then The Donald came on the scene. Trump captured the angry voters on the right. And what were Republicans angry about? They felt let down by the Republican establishment which they felt betrayed them and made deals with Big Government politicians. They were angry at President Obama ("not one of us") and felt "the others" were taking over. They were upset that everyone but they were benefitting from the economic recovery, they were mad at immigrants, Muslims, and "them." Donald Trump channeled their anger, amplified it, and gave voice to it. Responding to the surprising rise of the Donald, Jeb at first discounted Trump, then pursued a tortoise-and-hare approach, and when that too did not dislodge Trump as leader of the pack, he tried—unsuccessfully—to be an attack dog. But nothing worked. The Donald could not be stopped.

Trump appealed to the average citizen and was loathed by the Republican donor class. His "affluenza" became an asset, as he played the part of celebrity demagogue flying above politics as usual.

WE'RE IN THE MONEY: THE GREEN PRIMARY

To have a shot at the nomination, candidates have to play the big money game, making even the best of the candidates merely the "cleanest dirty shirt in the laundry hamper." The early search for big money is called the "Green Primary," and only those who can raise big money are taken seriously. Because of this, the donor class wields significant power. And money may also undermine democracy by creating a "weighted vote." John gives his vote plus $100 to candidate A. Mary gives her vote plus $100,000 to candidate B. Clearly Mary's vote carriers more weight? What do we "know" of the impact of money on presidential elections?

1. Money is important, but does not always guarantee victory—as Jeb Bush found out in 2016.
2. Not having big money seems to guarantee defeat. Search hard for a successful candidate who did not have access to big money.

3. Wealthy individuals can thus make their way in the race. Steve Forbes and Donald Trump are prime examples of this.

4. Dialing for Dollars. Money serves as a gatekeeper. Candidates are forced to spend a great deal of time raising money, and such money comes with strings attached.

5. Social Media and Money. An outsider (Sanders in 2015) can sometimes raise enough money to become a credible candidate using the Internet and social media.

6. Independent/Outside money allows for "dark money" to corrupt or influence the selection process.[1] Untraceable money raises suspicions of backroom deals and the buying of politicians.

The road to campaign finance reform has been a rocky one, and as of now, big money is in the driver's seat. In 1972, in *Bullock v. Carter*, the Supreme Court ruled that a person's economic status should not be an impediment in seeking elected office. This case struck down a Texas law that established "filing fees" (sometimes up to $8,900 to get placed on the ballot). Today, after a series of "money-liberating" decisions, the Supreme Court has landed us at the opposite end of the *Bullock* decision.

The "entry cost" for getting into the race today is generally over $1 billion. This hurdle discourages many considering a run in the first place. Only wealthy individuals (Mitt Romney or Donald Trump) or those willing to invest time—and perhaps compromise their principles—in extensive fundraising need apply for the job of president. In 2016, Trump donated $66 million of his own money to the campaign, in addition to raising another $280 million; Clinton raised $1.2 billion.

Candidates can form super PACs (political action committees) that can accept unlimited donations. There was a time when candidates went out of their way to avoid even the appearance of any financial impropriety. Today it is open season in the money race. What once were blurred lines have now all but been erased. We now have an "anything goes, Wild West" attitude about fundraising.

Competition for billionaire backers is fierce, and this donor primary precedes the actual primary and caucus season. The goal is to catch a billionaire so you can stay in the race. Fail to snare a big financial fish, and one's campaign is in trouble.

In the 2012 Republican primaries, a new "billionaire boys club" of mega donors became a key force in the selection process when casino mogul Sheldon Adelson bankrolled former House Speaker Newt Gingrich in his nomination bid. Adelson's money kept Gingrich in the race, even though Gingrich attracted very few voters.[2]

With the rise of billionaire donors and "dark money" (where donors' names are undisclosed), average citizens are both being spent out of the system and kept in the dark about who is donating to whom.[3]

Raising such large sums of money can be a compromising and sometimes corrupting process. Having to raise millions for a presidential race is at the heart of why some able people do not consider running for the presidency. It is also at the heart of why many people are turned off by the political process. At what point does a political contribution become a bribe? The late Hubert H. Humphrey, who twice ran unsuccessfully for president said:

> Campaign financing is a curse. It's the most disgusting, demeaning, disenchanting, debilitating experience of a politician's life. It's stinky. It's lousy. I just can't tell you how much I hate it. I've had to break off in the middle of trying to make a decent, honorable campaign and go up to somebody's parlor or to a room and say, "Gentlemen, and ladies, I'm desperate. You've got to help me...

...And you see people—a lot of them you don't want to see. And they look at you, and you sit there and you talk to them and tell them what you're for and you need help and, out of the twenty-five who have gathered, four will contribute. And most likely one of them is in trouble and is somebody you shouldn't have had a contribution from.[4]

Being forced to rely on big money makes the selection process vulnerable to charges of corruption. After the Watergate scandal in the 1970s, Congress passed legislation for public financing of presidential elections. This campaign-finance reform effort called for public disclosure of contributions exceeding one hundred dollars, established ceilings on contributions, created a system of federal subsidies, and established spending limits. In *Buckley v. Valeo* (424 U.S. 1, 1976) the Supreme Court determined that while the Congress could regulate contributions and expenditures of campaign organizations, it could not prevent or limit independent individuals or groups from exercising "free speech" rights.

Congress then passed the Federal Election Campaign Act (FECA), an effort to revise existing laws and keep them in line with new constitutional standards. The new guidelines have been in effect since the 1976 presidential election, but since that election, campaign organizations have discovered loopholes that allow campaigns to get around the law.

First, the "independent money" exemption allows individuals and organizations to spend money for or against candidates as long as their work is not coordinated by a candidate or their campaign organization. This allowed for "independent" spending on behalf of a candidate, or, more likely, negative campaign ads against a candidate. Second, the spending of "soft money" allowed party organizations to raise and spend money in support of the campaign.[5]

A major change occurred in 2010 when the Supreme Court,

in a 5-4 decision in the case *Citizens United v. Federal Election Commissions*, overruled campaign-spending precedents by allowing corporations and labor unions to contribute money to political campaigns. Arguing that *corporations* have the same rights as *persons*, the Court asserted that the First Amendment rights of free speech (which included money) apply to corporations and that the government may not ban political spending by corporations in elections. The Court's majority argued that their decision was a vindication of the First Amendment's basic free-speech right. Dissenters on the Court warned that unleashing corporate money would corrupt democracy. Additionally, the Court failed to account for the fact that many corporations are partially owned by foreign companies and individuals—a violation of U.S. law.[6]

The *Citizens United* decision marked a significant shift in the Supreme Court's approach, overruling two precedents. Up to that point the Court decided in *Austin v. Michigan Chamber of Commerce* (1990)[7] and *McConnell v. Federal Election Commission* (2003)[8] that corporate and labor campaign contributions could be restricted. The recent decisions overturning these cases were major victories for Republicans and big businesses.[9]

This led to the growth of super PACs. These Super PACs are supposed to be "independent" of individual candidates, yet the line is often blurred.

Is There A Citizens United Oligarchy?

A small number of donors have a big impact in funding presidential campaigns. Less than one percent of the top one percent donated in the United States more than one half of the money raised in the 2016 presidential primary campaign. Most of that money went to super PACs pledged to individual candidates. Twelve and a half million of the $16 million raised by Florida Senator Macro Rubio's PAC,

Conservative Solutions, came from just four donors. Texas Senator Ted Cruz raised $37 million, almost all of it from just three families. The largest donation to New Jersey Governor Chris Christie's PAC came from a single Boston investor (who wanted to a build a $4 billion-dollar resort in New Jersey). Over 80 percent of former Texas Governor Rick Perry's money for his short-lived campaign came from just three donors. More than half Rand Paul's money was provided by two donors.[10]

The green primary also allows fringe candidates (those with little popular support but big donor contributions) to wage a long campaign, staying in the race long after any hope of winning has been exhausted. The Supreme Court also opened the door to big money in campaigns with the 2014 decision in *McCutcheon v. Federal Election Commission.* In another 5-4 vote, the Court equated *money* with *speech* (as opposed to property). By deciding that money was speech, the Court gutted campaign finance restrictions, striking down the limits on how much a person could donate to a candidate per election cycle.

Although both liberal (DreamWorks CEO Jeffrey Katzenberg gave $3 million to Priorities USA Action) and conservative (the Koch brothers gave over $200 million to Americans for Prosperity) Super PACs have sprung up, overall spending in 2012 and 2016 was heavily in favor of Republicans.

To put U.S. campaign spending into perspective, the 2010 general election in Great Britain cost roughly $130 million for all its races. The U.S. 2012 presidential race alone cost roughly $3 billion; in 2016 it cost roughly $2 billion. Campaign contributions are often seen as investments in the future; and contributors often expect, and often do get, a return on their investments.

Increasingly, campaigns are utilizing the Internet in the race for the White House. YouTube did not exist in 2004, but in 2008 and 2016 it had a significant impact on the presidential contest. In addition to being a "first-stop-shopping" source for "gotcha" video clips, campaigns consciously utilized access to YouTube to get their message out, especially to young voters.[11]

New campaign technologies have dramatically changed both the way campaigns are conducted and how citizens connect to the campaign and the candidate.[12] These new technologies give us more quantity, but do they give us more quality? As new forms of social media rise, interest in "serious" news has declined.[13]

THE RACE HEATS UP

The Jeb and Hillary show quickly became the Donald and Bernie show. Two outsiders who appealed to the growing anger and resentment in the two parties. Sanders attacked privilege; Trump attacked, well, just about everyone.

A review of all the people and groups Trump attacked would take many pages. Suffice to say, he got mileage out of attacking illegal immigrants (calling them criminal and rapists) and war heroes (John McCain), declaring his wish to build a wall (that Mexico would somehow pay for) banning all Muslims from entering the United States (for an unspecified time), and bringing back the use of torture on suspected terrorists ("I will waterboard, and far worse").[14] His campaign theme "Make America Great Again" said little about how he planned to do it.

August 5, 2015, was the first Republican candidate debate. It was the most-watched primary debate in U.S. history. Why? Everyone wanted to see The Donald. And he did not disappoint. Trump dominated the stage, and no single rival emerged. And then the crowded field began to narrow. Texas Governor Rick Perry dropped out, soon followed by Wisconsin Governor Scott Walker, then

Louisiana Governor Bobby Jindal, and one by one they all began to fall away. The race seemed to belong to Trump.

February 1, 2016, the Iowa caucus, was the first test of the candidates. Texas Senator Ted Cruz barely beat Trump. The results were:

Ted Cruz 27.6%
Donald Trump 24.3%
Marco Rubio 23.1%
Ben Carson 9.3%
Rand Paul 4.5 %
Jeb Bush 2.8%

Trump lost! Cruz's narrow victory meant that Trump might be vulnerable, beatable.

On the Democratic side it was another close race with Clinton at 49.9% and Sanders at 49.6%. Clinton too seemed beatable.

Attention quickly turned to New Hampshire, and the first of a long list of primary elections. On February 4, Trump made his comeback:[15]

Donald Trump 35.3%
John Kasich 15.8%
Ted Cruz 11.7%
Jeb Bush 11.0%
Marco Rubio 10.6%

Rick Santorum, Carly Fiorina, Rand Paul, Mike Huckabee, George Pataki, and a few other Republicans dropped out. For the Democrats, it proved to be Bernie Sanders' night.

Bernie Sanders 60.4%

Hillary Clinton 38.0%

The race was on. And then, a fly fell into the ointment. Former New York City mayor, billionaire Michael Bloomberg threatened to run as an Independent if Trump and Sanders won the nominations of the parties. This could get very messy (and interesting).

Just after the New Hampshire primary, Supreme Court Justice Antonin Scalia passed away. Scalia one of the two most conservative Justices of the Court was appointed by Ronald Reagan. Hours after it was announced that Scalia had passed away, Republican Senate majority leader Mitch McConnell ruled out replacing Scalia until the next president was sworn in. Overnight, the 2016 election also became a decision about the ideological direction of the Court.

And Then There Were Five

The South Carolina primaries (February 20 for the Republicans; February 27 for the Democrats) narrowed the field and gave a sense of who was headed for the nomination. For the Republicans:[16]

> Donald Trump 32.5%
> Marco Rubio 22.5%
> Ted Cruz 22.3%
> Jeb Bush 7.8%
> John Kasich 7.6%
> Ben Carson 7.2%

As for the Democrats, Clinton crushed Sanders, placing her in the driver's seat on the road to the nomination with Clinton at 73.5% and Sanders at 26.0%.[17]

Although Jeb Bush had more recognition, experience, and access to significant money, he also had the albatross of his brother's presidency. Gobbled up and spit out by the Trump phenomenon, against which he had no strategy and no answer, Jeb raised nearly $160 million and did not win a single state. He regularly polled in single digits and was the butt of constant Trump jokes (Jeb is "low energy").[18]

To counter the toxic nature of the Bush brand, he ran merely as "Jeb!" It got him nowhere. And then he received a mixed blessing and had his brother, George W. Bush, campaign for him. Again, nothing. It got so bad that at one New Hampshire rally, Jeb had to ask the crowd, "Please clap."[19] In a year of the outsider, the candidate whom many saw as being representative of the Republican establishment had to suspend his campaign.

At the Republican debate in Houston, Texas, on February 25, things began to go downhill. In an effort to make up for his poor performance in the previous debate, and hoping to make up ground on frontrunner Donald Trump, Senator Marco Rubio went on the offensive, directly and repeatedly attacking Trump to devastating effect. Rubio repeatedly mocked and humiliated Trump which meant that Trump, bloodied by Rubio's attacks, began to counterattack.[20]

While entertaining, the display of petulance on the part of both Rubio and Trump made a mockery of the selection process. These were candidates seeking the presidency of the United States, they weren't auditioning for a part on *Jersey Shore*.[21] Trump had shaken things up so much that all the Republican frontrunners were now following his attack style. The campaign had descended into a circus.

Things went further downhill—for Trump at least—when in a February 28 interview with CNN, Trump refused to disavow an endorsement from David Duke, former Grand Dragon of the Ku Klux Klan, nor would he condemn the Klan itself. Later in the day Trump tried to pedal back on his earlier remarks, but the outcry against Mr. Trump was deafening.[22]

Over the course of the campaign, Trump had said a number of controversial things, including calling for a temporary ban on all Muslims entering the country,[23] repeatedly insulting Mexicans,[24] and making degrading comments toward women.[25] But none of these seemed to have any impact on his base, who seemed to love him more as he engaged in bombast and insults. But could—and would—the Republicans face the Democrats in November with the Trump brand heading the ticket? It took only two days to find out.

On March 1, "Super Tuesday," when a dozen states and territories held primaries and caucuses, Trump and Clinton emerged as the winners, but they failed to run the table and so their opponents remained in the race.

Trump won seven states, Cruz three, and Rubio one; this left Trump with a delegate total of 315, far short of the 1237 needed to clinch the nomination. Clinton won seven states, and Sanders four. Clinton was less than halfway to the needed delegated total of 2383. For the "Dump Trump" team, the strategy remained the same: win a few states here, a few there, and deny Trump a first ballot victory, then throw the choice to the convention. As a possible signal to what was ahead, overall turnout for the Democrats was down, but high for the Republicans. Was Trump, as he claimed, really bringing new voters back into the process?

The Republican establishment—and the pundit class—was slow to awaken to the Trump threat, but now, his victory was a real possibility. Trump was one step away from a hostile takeover of the Republican Party. He was a different sort of candidate. His main approach was to attack anyone in his way viciously. He played by his own rules, and shook up the establishment. And his followers loved it.

In February and March, egged on by Donald Trump who announced that he would pay the legal fees of supporters who beat up protesters ("I promise you," he said, "I will pay for the legal fees"),[26] things began to go downhill. The crowd at the Trump rally in Cedar Rapids, Iowa on February 1, 2016 went wild. Then, Trump supporters took The Donald's words seriously and started beating up anti-Trump protesters at rallies. Trump toned down some of his language, but the ugliness and violence at his rallies continued.

In early March, Dr. Ben Carson dropped out of the Republican race. Did this also clear the path for Trump? In the March 15 primaries, the nomination came closer to resolution. Hillary Clinton swept the table, winning Ohio, Illinois, Florida, North Carolina, and Missouri, taking her closer to the nomination. On the Republican side, Donald Trump won in North Carolina and Missouri, as well as in Rubio's home state of Florida, losing only Ohio to John Kasich, the state's governor. The Dump Trump movement could deny Trump the nomination only if he were to come in without the 1237 delegates needed to secure victory.

On the Democrat side, Bernie Sanders seemed unsinkable. He won races in Washington, Hawaii, and Alaska, closing the delegate gap with Clinton but still needing two-thirds of the remaining delegates to secure the nomination. While Sanders had momentum, Clinton continued to face questions about her use of e-mails while she was Secretary of State.

By early March, the Republican field narrowed to four and saw a switch in who and how money was being used. Traditionally, Republican-based "independent groups" spent vast sums of money attacking Democratic opponents. But in March, conservatives were attacking conservative candidates. These supposedly "independent" organizations used "dark money" (money that is collected but donor lists remain secret) to influence election outcomes. In the important Florida primary on March 15, ads appeared attacking Donald Trump as a fraud. These ads came not from Democrats but from the American Future Fund which spent millions of dollars in untraceable funds influencing politics. Groups like the American Future Fund sprang up after the Supreme Court's *Citizens' United* decision which allowed such nonprofits to raise and spend unlimited amounts of money, while keeping secret the names of donors. We know Republicans are savaging Republicans,[27] we just don't know who is doing the attacking. Of course, secrecy is the whole point of dark money—to keep people in the dark.

On March 3, in a lead editorial titled "Trump: Unfit to be President," the *Los Angeles Times* noted that "Much of the Republican base has taken leave of its senses," calling Trump a "cartoon character," and accusing him of being a "racist and a bully, a demagogue."[28] Newspapers and magazines around the world expressed shock and disappointment that someone so strange and racist might actually win the nominations of one of America's political parties. Max Hastings, writing in the *Daily Mail* (United Kingdom) wondered how a lying, racist, billionaire who called for a "jihad against Muslims and a trade war with China," could ever be taken seriously.[29] A *New York Times* article in mid-March found that 60 percent of Republicans were "mostly embarrassed" by the party's campaign.[30]

By March the Republican primary had devolved into little more than exchanging insults and seeing who could descend further, faster, and deeper into the gutter. Ted Cruz supporters tweeted semi-nude Melania Trump photos from a magazine. Trump tweeted split-screen images of Heidi Cruz with an unflattering expression next to a picture of Melania with the caption: "No need to 'spill the beans,' the images are worth a thousand words." Trump supporters threatened to out Cruz for multiple martial indiscretions. The key issues for the Republican candidates seemed to be who had the bigger "hands" and who had the hottest wife. And yes, one of these men was the likely Republican nominee for President of the United States.

Trump's incendiary rhetoric about beating up protesters at his rallies and offering to pay the legal fees of his supporters who were charged with assault, came home to roost when, on March 29, Trump's campaign manager Corey Lewandowski was arrested and charged with battery against news reporter Michelle Fields of the Conservative-leaning Breitbart News.[31] While Lewandowski asserted that he never touched the reporter, video evidence suggested otherwise (the case was later dropped).

The seeds of Trump's calls to violence—intermixed with claims that he was against such violence—were drawn directly into the center of Trump's campaign. The 2016 Republican "hold your nose" primary couldn't get more bizarre, or could it?

For 2016, Donald Trump's campaign was largely self-funded. Hillary Clinton was able to build a large war-chest early, while Bernie Sanders used the Internet to accumulate a large amount of smaller donations, which built up as the momentum of his campaign grew. Ted Cruz initially was dependent on a few large donors, and John Kasich ran on a tight budget and thus was limited in his outreach.

RACE AND CLASS

While often considered taboo subjects, race and class became important topics in the 2016 contest. Race had played an important, though largely hidden, part in the Obama presidency as critics tried to portray him as the "other" and "not one of us," coupled with the Trump-led Birther movement and angry demands to "take back our country." In 2016, the race card and racism were prominent features on the campaign trail as first Trump, and later Cruz, were openly hostile to Mexicans, Muslims (Trump), and American Muslims (Cruz).[32] What used to be coded messages uttered in a "race dog whistle" form, became open bullhorn messages. Spouting racist pleas was now apparently acceptable.

Class, too played a part as both the Democratic and Republican sides. For the Democrats, Bernie Sanders used as a central component of his message, a call to revolution against the 1%. And most of Trump's followers were white middle-class males who felt stuck in dead-end jobs with stagnant wages. Trump was their savior against the millionaire class. Both racial and class resentments openly played a role in the 2016 contest for the presidency.

BACK TO THE CAMPAIGN

Due to his celebrity status and bombastic style, Donald Trump received a great deal more free air time than did any of his rivals. Cable news channels often broadcast his speeches at rallies, in the hopes of capturing a "Trump Moment" when his rhetoric went over the top, or his lack of policy knowledge stumped him. Trump made for great TV. In fact, according to MEDIAQUANT, Trump received $189.80 worth of free coverage for every dollar he spent on paid advertising.[33]

Ted Cruz also hung on in the race. The Texas senator emerged in April and May as the only alternative to Trump, and in late March when Trump imploded over his flubs on answering questions about abortion, the momentum shifted from "Stop Trump" to "Elect Ted" mode. The irony here is that while Trump had negatives that topped all the other candidates, Cruz wasn't far behind. Ted Cruz was strongly disliked by the Republican mainstream for his "doesn't play well with others" self-centeredness.[34] But Trump who at first seemed impervious to criticism, found that after flip-flop or flub, the mistakes started to stick and criticism grew, and by early April, Trump's negatives had "played to an unequaled low"[35] and—if he won the nomination— "would be the most unpopular nominee in the history of U.S. opinion surveys."[36] And "by a lot" added pollster Peter Hart. Trump's negatives were at 68 percent.[37]

In late April the Dump Trump forces, fearing that Trump would be able to win enough delegates to secure a first-ballot convention victory, decided to join forces against Trump. Ted Cruz and John Kasich agreed to coordinate their efforts to deny Trump a first-ballot win, with each candidate stepping aside in chosen races in hopes the other could garner enough votes to stop Trump. Cruz was to go it alone in Indiana, and Kasich would be the standard bearer in Oregon and New Mexico.

As the Cruz-Kasich effort to join forces to Dump Trump fizzled, Cruz tried yet another desperate Hail Mary pass when, on April 21, he announced that if nominated, he would select California businesswoman Carly Fiorina as his running mate. It didn't work. Nothing seemed to work against the Trump juggernaut.

Trying to meet criticism that his public policy proposals were no more than "policy-lite,"[38] and trying to counter an open letter by more than a hundred conservative Republican foreign policy experts who expressed horror over Trump's incoherent and reckless foreign policy pronouncements,[39] on April 27 Trump delivered a foreign-policy address (uncharacteristically reading from a teleprompter). Proposing an "America First" approach, Trump promised a foreign policy "that replaces randomness with purpose, ideology with strategy, and chaos with peace."[40]

Advertised as the first of several speeches devoted to policy, Trump's first venture into serious policy left most people disappointed.[41] Full of platitudes and paradoxes, the speech raised more questions than it answered, and served only to reinforce the view that on matters of policy, Trump was clueless.[42]

Some thought that the wheels would come off the Trump bus when Trump said, during an April MSNBC interview with Chris Matthews, that women who had abortions should be "punished."[43] This created a two-news-cycle storm, but in the end, Trump's supporters just didn't seem to care about The Donald's policy positions as much as they were captivated by the Trump persona.

As exciting as the Republican primary was, the Democratic race seemed to match it in dullness. Hillary Clinton exercised on "attrition warfare" approach, compiling a large war chest of money, big-name endorsements, and relying on a big early lead to win the nomination. The surprisingly effective challenge by Bernie Sanders, who enlivened young voters and also amassed a large war chest from relatively small donors, gave Clinton a run for her money until May when attrition warfare won the day. But not before Sanders turned a bit nasty, as his principled positions gave way to increasingly personal attacks, going so far as to assert that he did not believe that Mrs. Clinton was not qualified to be president.[44] Still Clinton held the lead.

While clearly the frontrunner, and with repeated calls from allies and Republican elites to act "more presidential," Trump nonetheless continued to spout birther-like absurdities. In early May, on Fox News, Trump, taking his cue from a story in the tabloid *National Enquirer* (the "newspaper" that produced headlines such as Supreme Court Justice Antonin Scalia was murdered by a hooker),[45] said that it was "horrible" that Ted Cruz's father was an associate of John F. Kennedy's assassin Lee Harvey Oswald.[46] How could Trump get away with such filth and not suffer electorally? Had the voters descended into reality-television world, where the crazier the better was the order of the day? Former George W. Bush speechwriter Michael Gerson warned that

> The standards and values of reality-television - the exaggerated feuds, the personal vilification, and the deleted expletives - have invaded the political realm. And it is a form of social decay. It is good manners that allow citizens to argue with coming to blows, and even to find productive compromise. In most everyday circumstances, manners matter more than laws. Good manners involve an affirmation that we, all of us, are part of the same community, and that everyone is due a certain minimal amount of respect. Poor manners, in

contrast, can indicated the dehumanization of individuals and groups. The boor is often the bigot.[47]

Ted Cruz responded to Trump's implying that Cruz's father might be implicated in the JFK assassination with an all-out attack on Trump. Defending his father, Cruz went on to call Trump "a pathological liar, utterly amoral," and as "narcissistic." He further said that Trump was a man "for whom morality does not exist," that Trump is "terrified of strong women," and that he, Trump, openly bragged how "great it is to commit adultery." Cruz wasn't finished. He mocked Trump's statement that conquering "venereal disease was his personal Vietnam,"[48] and that Trump was a "serial philanderer and boasts about it." Did anyone care or was Trump the celebrity with Teflon coating, a celebrity who just might be the next President of the United States?

Trump won in Indiana, and Cruz dropped out. The next day, Kasich too dropped out. There was no stopping Trump now. Could he unite the party? Could he reduce his high "negatives"? Could he appeal to women? Could he win? Could he possibly become the next President of the United States?

It was down to two. Trump versus Clinton. A flamboyant, politically inexperienced billionaire who during the primaries seemed like a racist, sexist bully, against a very politically experienced but flat campaigner who was weighted down by much baggage. In a year of anti-Washington sentiment, could the novice outsider appeal to enough angry voters to win the election?

Trump and Clinton had secured the nominations but the irony is that both candidates had astronomically high negative ratings. A Roper Center poll from April found Trump to have the highest "strongly unfavorable" rating of any candidate since 1980.[49] Hillary Clinton had the second highest negative rating. It was shaping up to be a brutal contest between two of the most disliked figures in American politics. And if things got down and dirty, it was advantage Trump. The Donald won the Republican primary by attacking his opponents viciously. During the primaries Trump likened opponent Ben Carson to a pedophile,[50] implied that Ted Cruz's wife was ugly,[51] cited the *National Enquirer* as his source linking Ted Cruz's father to the Kennedy assassination,[52] and the list goes on and on.

According to the conventional wisdom, after securing the party nomination, a candidate should 1) solidify the base; 2) try to expand from the base; 3) select key battleground states that had to be won in order to gain victory in the general election. But Trump was anything but conventional.

Both Clinton and Trump began their campaign with high unfavorable ratings, and the campaigns reinforced and amplified these negative views. Clinton and Trump did not rise in favorability as the campaigned progressed; they got more *unpopular*. By election time, Clinton had an over 40% unfavorable rating while Trump registered over 50%.[53]

For Trump, the endorsements were not coming in. Mitt Romney, the party's nominee in the previous election refused to endorse him, as did Republican Senator Lindsey Graham and Ben Sasse. House Speaker Paul Ryan said he was just not ready to endorse. Jeb Bush said he wouldn't vote for the candidate.

Securing the nomination was difficult enough for Donald Trump, but putting the party back together was probably harder. Several prominent Republicans, including George H. W., George W. Bush, and Romney, refused to support Trump. This marked the first time since 1912, when Theodore Roosevelt refused to endorse (and even ran against) William Howard Taft, that a party's previous nominee refused to endorse the current nominee. Some prominent Republicans even went as far as to search for an Independent /

Republican "third-party" candidate to oppose Trump. With party unity in jeopardy, down-ticket Republicans (i.e., those running for Senate or Congress) worried Trump might take them down with him.

In early June, as a triumphant Trump tried to unite the Republicans behind his candidacy, the thin-skinned candidate got into trouble with leaders in his own party over when on several occasions, he ventured off message and began attacking the federal judge hearing a fraud lawsuit against Trump University. Trump asserted that because the judge was Mexican (who was actually born in Indiana), there was a conflict of interest because the judge was inherently unable to be fair to Trump, and should therefore recuse himself from the case. Trump repeated his attack on several different occasions and, even when given the opportunity to retract these remarks, refused to back down.[54]

Illinois Republican Senator Mark Kirk then withdrew his endorsement of Trump. South Carolina Republican Senator Lindsey Graham announced he would not vote for Trump, and House Majority Paul Ryan called Trump's attack on the judge "the textbook definition of a racist."[55] Republicans were quickly abandoning the seemingly sinking Trump ship. Could Trump put a plug in this crack?

And what would Bernie Sanders do? As the primary season approached the end line, Sanders kept insisting he would take his case all the way to the convention. But with the race already sewn up in early June, prolonging the race seemed fruitless and dangerous. Clinton needed Sanders's young voters, but they wouldn't let go of their hopes of Sanders becoming the Democratic candidate. Might Sanders be the 2016 version of Ralph Nader in 2000, when Nader drained enough votes from Al Gore in Florida to deliver the presidency to George W. Bush?

The June 7 Super Tuesday primaries put Hillary Clinton over the top. She had more than enough committed delegates to be widely seen as the Party's presumptive nominee. It was a historic night. Eight years earlier the United States elected an African American president. Now, for the first time, a woman would receive the nomination for president from one of the two major parties.

The race was on: Donald Trump versus Hillary Clinton. Everyone expected the race to be down and dirty, and it was.

DID TRUMP HAVE THE MEDIA IN HIS BACK POCKET?

A study done by Harvard University's Shorenstein Center on Media, Politics, and Public Policy looked at media coverage of the primary season, focusing on eight leading news outlets (*New York Times, LA Times, Washington Post, Wall Street Journal, USA Today*, CBS, NBC, and Fox News). It concluded that "news coverage.... strongly boosted Donald Trump's bid and put Hillary Clinton at a disadvantage," adding that "from the time he announced his run in mid-June 2015 to the end of the year, Trump received about one-third of all coverage of the Republican race among 17 candidates," and that coverage "was overwhelmingly favorable."[56] Trump received about twice the coverage as early favorite, Florida's ex-governor Jeb Bush. It was estimated that Trump got $55 million of free publicity to Bush's $20 million. By contrast, stories about Hillary Clinton "overwhelmingly took a negative tone."[57]

HOW FAR WOULD TRUMP GO?

On June 12, in Orlando, Florida, Omar Mateen went into the Pulse nightclub, a venue frequented by members of the LGBTQ community, and opened fire with an AR-15 semi-automatic rifle. Before Mateen was killed by Orlando, Florida police, he had killed more than fifty people. Reactions to this tragedy varied, but nowhere was the contrast between Trump and Clinton better revealed than in the way these two potential presidents reacted to this tragedy.

Clinton spoke of the post 9/11 tragedy and how Americans—Democrats and Republicans—pulled together, worked together, and united as one nation. She expressed condolences for the victims and their families, condemned the attack as an act of terrorism, and reached out to the LGBTQ community with expressions of support.[58]

Trump sent out a tweet (9:43 AM) "Appreciate the congrats for being right on radical Islamic terrorism; I don't want congrats, I want toughness and vigilance. We must be smart."[59] Even in the face of tragedy, it was all about Trump. The self-congratulatory Trump seemed narcissistic, self-absorbed, and out of touch with the pain of others.

People started to ask: which one do I want to be president when crises come? Their clashing styles were brought to the fore in this crisis, and the contrast was stunning. Trump made matters worse by using the tragedy to attack President Obama, saying, "he doesn't get it, or he gets it better than anybody understands."[60] Shortly thereafter he dug a deeper hole for himself saying that President Obama "is not tough, not smart—or he's got something else in mind."[61]

The following day the *Los Angeles Times* editorialized that "Trump's shoot-from-the-hip persona makes him unsuited for the presidency…" and expressed the hope that he would be sent packing at the election and that he "takes his repugnant intolerance with him."[62]

Shortly after securing the nomination, rather than securing his Republican base, one by one Republicans were distancing themselves from the presumptive nominee. Talk of a "Dump Trump" coup at the Cleveland Convention continued, and a type of "buyer's remorse" seemed to set in.

Republican office-holders, as well as rank-and-file Republicans began to peel away from Trump. Shortly after, some major donors followed suit. Several large corporations announced they would not—as is customary and expected—help fund the July Republican Convention in Cleveland. Apple announced that due to Trump's prejudiced remarks, they were pulling out.[63] So did Wells Fargo,[64] United Parcel Service,[65] Motorola,[66] JP Morgan Chase,[67] Ford,[68] Walgreens,[69] and Hewlett Packard.[70] Coca-Cola reduced its funding from $660,000 in 2012 to just $75,000 in 2016.[71] Microsoft would provide tech support but unlike 2012 would not be giving any money.[72]

By mid-June, the general election campaign had begun. In traditional campaign terms, Hillary Clinton was way ahead of Trump in fundraising and in campaign organization—both essential to develop an effective "ground game." But this was not a traditional campaign.

The Clinton general election campaign hit the ground running. Due to their huge lead in having money on hand, the Clinton team was able to air a series of television ads in key states designed to do two things: 1) cast Clinton in a favorable light; and 2) expose Trump as inexperienced, intemperate, and volatile. By reaching the voters before Trump, Clinton sought to frame the campaign themes on her terms and present voters with a comparison of the two rivals in ways that favored Clinton.

This came at a time when Trump's "negatives" were on the rise. A *Washington Post/ABC News* poll from mid-June found that 7 in 10 voters had a negative impression of Trump, with 50% who feel "strongly" unfavorable. Hillary Clinton's 55% negative ratings, while high, contrasted favorably with Trump's deep favorability hole. Broken down, 77% of women had an unfavorable view of Trump (47% for Clinton); 94% of African Americans and 89% of Hispanics had an unfavorable view of Trump. The one "bright" spot for Trump was that 68% of white voters had a favorable view of the candidate.[73]

E-MAIL FIASCO

Throughout the primary campaign, one issue hounded Clinton: her e-mails. The Federal Bureau of Investigation (FBI) was conducting an investigation into the use of her personal, unsecured e-mail server while she served as Secretary of State. Were classified materials improperly handled? Did she break the law? Would she be indicted?

On July 5, FBI director James Comey announced that he would not recommend criminal charges against Clinton. He was also highly critical of Clinton's "extremely careless" use of classified and sensitive material.[74]

It was good news for the Clinton team that there was no indictment. But Comey's devastating critique of the sloppy and careless practice of Clinton's e-mail use did her great damage. For Clinton, as with her husband eighteen year ago, the Republicans took a strong case against her, and so mishandled it that her enemies came in to save her. The Republicans, in their pursuit for an indictment, let the real story—that Clinton was sloppy and careless—go by as they railed against director Comey as he testified before Congress. Comey (a lifelong Republican and former assistant attorney general under George W. Bush) sliced the Republicans to shreds. Comey's smackdown of Trey Gowdy of South Carolina left the congressman stunned and silent.[75] Had the Republicans just saved Clinton's campaign?

While FBI Director James Comey did not recommend that any criminal charges be filed against Hillary Clinton, his report was nonetheless highly critical of Clinton's handling of her emails. Comey testified that Clinton was sloppy and careless about handing classified e-mails, and that her non-government, non-secure e-mail server might have been hacked.

THE CONVENTIONS

There was a time when national party conventions actually selected the party nominee. Yes, backroom-deals in smoke-filled rooms sometimes thwarted the will of the people, but more often, fairly capable, and electable candidates emerged from this behind-the-scenes process. The last time a convention actually selected a candidate was in 1952 when the Republican contest between party favorite Robert Taft and the people's favorite Dwight D. Eisenhower ended up with Eisenhower's nomination.

Today, because candidates arrive at the convention with a sufficient number of delegates (from primaries and caucuses) to guarantee their nomination, the convention resembles more a coronation than a contest. Today's conventions are part infomercial, part celebration, and if there is anything that occurs that is unscripted —that is a problem.

In the week prior to the Republican convention, Donald Trump made a particularly public display of his vice-presidential "dating game" selection process, with several key possibilities traveling to Indiana where Trump—and his children—interviewed the hopefuls.[76] In marched Mike Pence, Newt Gingrich, Chris Christie, and others to be assessed by Trump and his children.

In the end, Trump made the "safe" choice: Mike Pence, Indiana governor and former House member. Trump was still having trouble solidifying the conservative wing of the Republican Party; and Pence, a fiscal and social conservative, was to help reassure conservatives that yes, Trump is "one of us."

Less than twenty-four hours after Trump offered and Pence accepted the vice-presidential nomination, Trump got cold feet. Top staff members and Pence himself were openly talking about the Pence selection, yet at the same time, Trump—on Wednesday evening around midnight—called several of his key aides asking if it was too late to withdraw Pence's name.[77] The answer was no.

On Wednesday Mike Pence publicly acknowledged that Donald Trump had offered him the vice presidency.[78] But on Thursday night on Fox News, Trump said he had not yet decided.[79] Was this a lie or Trump waffling?

Word of the Trump flip-flop got out quickly as CNN and NBC and other news outlets were confirming Trump's confusion. Pence had already flown from Indiana to New York for the formal announcement. But Trump balked. Pence informed Trump that it was a done deal and that he fully expected to be Trump's running mate.[80] Trump's buyer's remorse suggested how messy and confused the Trump campaign was. In the end, Trump announced on Twitter that Pence would be his vice president.[81]

As Trump's running mate, Pence was a bland but positive choice. A man of impeccable conservative credentials, Pence was reassuring to the Republican Party right wing. His nomination was a signal to conservatives that they need not worry about Trump.

In his July 16 public announcement that Mike Pence would be his vice-presidential nominee, Trump repeatedly got off message. His script was a promotion of Pence and yet he kept drifting from script to talk about himself.[82] Question: was this a Trump weakness, or a Trump strength? Was his imperial ego the reason for his rise, or would it be the cause of his downfall?

In presenting his new VP choice to the public, Trump spent 29 minutes talking about himself before introducing Pence.[83] Contrast that with past Republican VP announcements: George W. Bush spoke for seven minutes then turned things over to Dick Cheney;[84] Mitt Romney spoke for 8 ½ minutes before turning things over to Paul Ryan.[85]

The Republican convention began on Monday, July 18, in Cleveland, Ohio. John Kasich, the state's Republican governor and Trump's former primary rival, refused to even attend the convention[86] (only 33% of the party's fifty-four U.S. Senators showed up at the convention;[87] with Arizona's Jeff Flake saying "I've got to mow my lawn,"[88] and Nebraska's Ben Sasse telling reporters he would be taking his children to "watch some dumpster fires across the state."[89] The "dump Trump" forces made a desperate last-ditch effort to stop the presumptive nominee, but that fizzled and faded by the end of day one.

From a distance, the convention looked like a sea of white. The delegates were a fairly old and an almost-exclusively white crowd. According to *Fusion*, of the Democratic Party's 4766 delegates, 2887 delegates were women, 1182 were African American, 747 Latinos, 633 LGBT, 292 Asian, and 147 were Native American.[90] By contrast, of the 2472 at the Republican Party Convention, 18 delegates (.73%) were African American.[91] As for diversity, the convention's version of diversity seemed to be rich, white males interacting with even richer white males. As for the glitz of star power, the A-list of Hollywood headliners speaking for Trump was led by Scott Baio[92] and Willie Robertson from the reality show *Duck Dynasty*.

At just before 4:00PM on the first day of the convention, the Republican National Committee (RNC), rushed through on voice vote only (with no debate), a rule (rule 39) that would have all but ended the dump Trump effort. Nine states formally demanded a roll-call vote (seven is the number of states necessary to compel —by RNC rules—a roll-call vote) on the rules. But the convention chair refused.[93]

Gordon Humphrey, former Republican Senator from New Hampshire, and an "anybody but Trump" advocate,[94] said the Republican leadership running the convention were "brownshirts" who were acting like fascists.[95] Former Virginia attorney general Ken

Cuccinelli told MSNBC, "They [the RNC] cheated."[96] The stop Trump forces failed to get the RNC to follow the rules they themselves had established. The road had been cleared for a Trump nomination. But what of party unity? After this melee, the Colorado state delegation walked out.

Monday started off with a bang as the floor fight over the convention rules failed to silence the stop Trump supporters. But by mid-evening, the convention morphed into a dump-on-Hillary-Clinton festival as speaker after speaker attacked Clinton for everything from Benghazi to her e-mails. But the highlight of the day was a speech by Donald Trump's third wife, Melania Trump, delivered with poise, grace, and somebody else's words. That somebody else was Michelle Obama.[97]

Just hours after Melania delivered her speech to rave reviews, word came out that she had lifted portions of her convention speech from Michelle Obama's 2008 convention speech.[98] Campaign head Paul Manafort wasted no time in throwing Melania under the bus as he tried to distance himself (and the speechwriter he assigned to work with Melania) from the debacle.[99]

Melania's speech was a gold-plated gift to late-night comedians and social media. The jokes flowed freely:

> Melania: Not only were the accusations of plagiarism hurtful to me, but they also hurt my children Sasha and Malia.[100]

> Opening of Melania's speech: "I was born a poor black child in Chicago..."[101]

Day two of the Republican Convention went much better for Trump. He was officially named the party's nominee, and the speeches by New Jersey Governor Chris Christie and Trump's eldest son Donald Trump Jr. were well received. But the plagiarism issue just wouldn't go away. The RNC and Trump campaign manager

Paul Manafort insisted that there was no plagiarism. And yet on Wednesday morning the campaign announced that a Trump company employee Meredith McIver did indeed plagiarize portions of Melania's speech from a Michelle Obama 2008 speech. The campaign chaos was becoming the story of the convention. Could they put the train back on the tracks?

To make things worse, on day three of the convention it was reported that the Secret Service was investigating one of Donald Trump's advisers, Al Baldasaro, after he called for the execution of Hillary Clinton. His exact quote, "Hillary Clinton should be put in the firing line and shot for treason."[102] Thus, as the convention continued, the Trump team, dazed and confused, couldn't get its act together. If they couldn't run a convention, how did they expect to run a government?

Things just kept getting worse for Trump as day three of the convention was supposed to be Mike Pence's opportunity to present himself to the American people as the ticket's vice-presidential pick. But Pence's solid speech was buried under the controversy that was Ted Cruz. Senator Cruz, still stinging from the Trump attack on Heidi Cruz, the Senator's wife (intimating in a tweet that she was ugly) and on Rafael Cruz, the Senator's father (suggesting in a tweet that he was somehow implicated in JFK's assassination), refused, in his prime-time convention speech to endorse Trump. Yet again, the Trump Team had lost control of the narrative, got off message, and appeared incompetent.

Could Trump give his flagging convention a reboot? The final day of the Republican Convention was a filler awaiting the star's performance. Daughter Ivanka Trump introduced her father to the convention and television-viewing public, hoping—with some success—to humanize him and present the soft, fuzzy side of Trump.

When Trump himself finally took to the podium, he delivered

a very long (one-hour and twenty minutes, longer than the 2012 Obama and Romney acceptance speeches combined) and a very dark, angry address. A *Los Angeles Times* article said, "It was a voice suffused with anger and steeped in resentment."[103]

Trump's convention speech was a surprisingly dark, almost apocalyptic portrayal of a country on the verge of collapse, and as he said, "I alone can fix it."[104] Arguing that the Democrats had left a legacy of "death, destruction, terrorism, and weakness," Trump promised to "liberate our citizens from the crime and terrorism and lawlessness that threatens their communities." But "beginning on January 20 of 2017, safety will be restored."[105]

Trump's speech was "I" and "me," but rarely "we." Only he, Trump said, could save America. So dark was his message that comedian Bill Maher joked that the speech was "so depressing that Melania started to plagiarize a suicide note."[106] The speech energized the crowd at the convention, but was the public ready to embrace such an apocalyptic vision?

And as was the case with the previous three days of the Republican Convention, day four was also a day of damage control for the Trump campaign as Paul Manafort and other Trump spokespersons had to explain away the controversial remarks Trump made in a *New York Times* interview in which he suggested that as president, he might not honor our NATO treaty obligations to our allies.[107] Blowback from this bizarre remark found both Democrats and Republicans condemning Trump for such a foolish and dangerous statement. Even Republican Senate Majority leader Mitch McConnell was tepid in his response to Trump's flub: "I am willing to kind of chalk it up to a rookie mistake."[108] But Trump, in typical Trump fashion, stood by his remarks.

The highlight of the Republican Convention? The speeches by the Trump children—Tiffany, Donald Jr., Eric, and Ivanka (Barron, age 10 did not speak) —were uniformly excellent and gave a boost to a convention high on flubs and low on quality.

Among the many flubs and fumbles of the Republican Convention perhaps the most worrisome was the anger, hatred, and resentment so evident in the crowd. The *Los Angeles Times* said the delegates were "reminiscent of a lynch mob" with their daily repetition of the convention mantra, "Lock Her Up." It wasn't pretty, it wasn't mature, and it wasn't appropriate.[109]

THE DEMOCRATS TAKE CENTER STAGE

As the Republican Convention came to a close, it was time for the Democrats to step forward. On Friday, July 22, Hillary Clinton announced that she had selected Virginia Senator Tim Kaine as her vice-presidential running mate.

Some on the left of the Party complained that Kaine just wasn't progressive enough; that they wanted Bernie Sanders or Elizabeth Warren to have been on the ticket. But such complaints aside, most hailed Kaine as a solid, safe, and positive pick.

Kaine, former mayor of Richmond, governor of Virginia, and sitting senator for that state, had solid progressive credentials, spoke fluent Spanish, had never lost an election, and came from a key battleground state. In their first joint appearance on Saturday July 23, Kaine gave a roaring speech that energized a large Florida crowd,[110] and gave a hint that his selection might strengthen the Democratic ticket—especially among a group that remained lukewarm to Hillary Clinton: the white, male, working-class voters.

Just before the start of the Democratic Convention in Philadelphia, a Russian hacker, claiming to be a part of WikiLeaks, released e-mails, which showed that during the primaries, the Democratic National Committee was—as Bernie Sanders claimed—favoring

Hillary Clinton. This embittered many of the Sanders supporters who were already threatening to disrupt the convention.

The DNC e-mail flop very quickly led to the resignation of Debbie Wasserman Schultz, Chairperson of the Democratic National Committee. It also gave ammunition to Sanders voters who were disinclined to vote for Clinton.

If the day started badly for the Democrats, they soon found their footing and the evening's convention addresses were uniformly excellent. From New Jersey Senator Cory Booker to Massachusetts progressive Senator Elizabeth Warren, from First Lady Michelle Obama, who gave the best speech of either convention, to Vermont Senator and nomination runner-up Bernie Sanders, it was an evening of rousing speeches—almost universally optimistic in tone, in sharp contrast to the doom-and-gloom speeches to the Republican Convention—all designed to unify a split party.

Day 3 of the Convention had barely gotten under way when Donald Trump tried to stir the hornet's nest by publicly inviting Russia (yes, Russia!) to hack into secure U.S. computers to try to find e-mails that might be embarrassing to Hillary Clinton.[111] Many wondered if Trump's strategy of colluding with an adversary had been an error in expression, but later in the day, when Trump was pressed to explain his remarks, he—once again—doubled down and said yes, he wanted Russia to find and release e-mails from when Hillary Clinton was Secretary of State.[112] The next day, however, Trump said it was all a joke, and that he was merely being "sarcastic."[113] Really?

What created a firestorm was the July 28 speech by Khizr Khan who flanked by the wife, spoke passionately and powerfully about the sacrifice of his son, Army Captain Humayan Khan, who was killed in Iraq in 2004 protecting his troops from a suicide bomber. Captain Khan's father served Trump with a major league smackdown about immigrants and Trump's positions on Muslims. "Have you ever read the U.S. Constitution?" he asked, and then pulled a pocket Constitution out of his jacket offering to "gladly lend my copy" to Trump.[114] Khan's short speech got Trump in a tizzy fit, one whose results would not become clear until after the convention.[115]

Once the Day 3 keynote speech started, the Democrats went full throttle into the pro-Clinton, anti-Trump speeches. Former New York Mayor Michael Bloomberg, an Independent, vice-presidential candidate Tim Kaine, Vice President Joe Biden, and President Barak Obama went full force in celebrating Hillary Clinton and attacking Donald Trump. Obama especially rounded off Day 3 with an exciting ending.

Day 4, the final day of the Democratic Convention was all buildup to Hillary Clinton's formal acceptance speech. Introduced by her daughter Chelsea, Clinton, not known as a rousing orator, gave a strong speech in which she not only noted the historical importance of the first woman ever nominated by a major party for president, but also drew stark contrasts between herself and Donald Trump on experience, temperament, and the vision for America's future. All in all, it was a very good convention for the Democrats, and they left Philadelphia not quite with party unity, but on a strong note nonetheless.

The nomination process for all its media attention and bluster, produced candidates selected by just 9 percent of the U.S. population, or 14 percent of all eligible adults.[116] For all the sound and fury, relatively few voters actually selected Trump and Clinton as the nominees.

NOTES

1. Jane Mayer, *Dark Money: The Hidden History of the Billionaires Behind the Rise of the Radical Right* (New York: Doubleday, 2016).
2. The Democrats have their own stable of billionaires, including environmental activists, who spent nearly $70 million in the 2014 mid-terms. And given the huge lead Hillary Clinton had in 2015, the big money donors were not as relevant in the more undecided Republican race.
3. John Nichols and Robert W. McChesney, *Dollarocracy* (New York: Nation Books, 2013); and Kenneth P. Vogel, *Big Money* (New York: Public Affairs, 2014).
4. Quoted in Thomas E. Cronin and Michael A. Genovese, *The Paradoxes of the American Presidency*, 4th ed. (New York: Oxford Press, 2012).
5. Anthony Gierzynski, *Money Rules* (Boulder: Westview, 2000).
6. The Foreign Agents Registration Act, 1966.
7. 494 U.S. 652. (1990).
8. 540 U.S. 93 (2003).
9. See Jane Mayer, "Attack Dog," *The New Yorker,* February 13&20, 2012, 40–49
10. Nicholas Confessore, Sarah Cohen, and Karen Yourish, "Small Pod of Rich Donors Dominates Election," *The New York Times,* August 1, 2015. While the number of doors is known, the names are not always available due to campaign financing rules that allow for dark money to be spent.
11. Virginia Heffernan, "Clicking and Choosing: The Election According to YouTube." *The New York Times Magazine* (November, 16, 2008), 22–24.
12. Richard L. Fox and Jennifer M. Ramos: *iPolitics Citizens, Governing, and Governing in the New Media Era* (New York: Cambridge University Press, 2012).
13. See Markus Prior, *Post-Broadcast Democracy* (New York: Cambridge University Press. 2007).
14. Kurtis Lee, "A Quick Guide to the People and Groups Donald Trump Has Insulted," *The Los Angeles Times,* February 18, 2016.

15. Stephen Collinson, "Outsiders Sweep to Victory in New Hampshire," *CNN: Politics*, February 10, 2016.
16. "South Carolina Primary: CNN/ORC Poll Full Results," *CNN Politics*, February 16, 2016.
17. Ibid.
18. Ed O'Keefe, "Jeb Bush Drops Out of 2016 Presidential Campaign," *The Washington Post*, February 20, 2016.
19. Ann Marie Awad, "Campaign 2016: Jeb Bush, Are You Okay?" *UPI*, February 3, 2016.
20. David A. Graham, "Donald Trump's Terrible Night," *The Atlantic*, February 25, 2016.
21. *Jersey Shore* is an American reality television series which ran on MTV. An article notes that "The brilliance of the show was its outrageousness." See http://www.complex.com/pop-culture/2016/10/jersey-shore-mtv-ranking/.
22. Glenn Kessler, "Donald Trump and David Duke: For the Reward," *The Washington Post*, March 1, 2016.
23. Jeremy Diamond, "Donald Trump: Ban all Muslim Travel to U.S.," *CNN Politics*, December 8, 2015.
24. Katie Reilly, "Here are All the Times Donald Trump Insulted Mexico," *TIME*, August 31, 2016.
25. Gregory Krieg, "Donald Trump's Trouble with Women – an Incomplete List," *CNN Politics*, September 28, 2016.
26. Clarence Page, "Is Trump to Blame for Violence at his Rallies? *Chicago Tribune*, April 18, 2017.
27. Karoli Kuns, "How Dark Money Shields Political Donors," *Newsweek*, June 30, 2015.
28. Editorial, "Trump: Unfit to be President," March 3, 2016, *Los Angeles Times*, A10.
29. See "Europe Panics Over Trump," *The Week*, March 11, 2016, 14.
30. See Patrick Healy and Megan Thee-Brenan, "Most Republicans Say '16 Race is Embarrassing," *New York Times*, March 22, 2016, A1.
31. David A. Graham, "Why Trump's Campaign Manager was Arrested for Battery," *The Atlantic*, March 29, 2016.
32. Ali Gharib, "Ted Cruz is an Anti-Muslim Bigot, too," *The Nation*, March 18, 2016.
33. Stephen Battaglio, "TV Town Halls a Winning Format," *The Los Angeles Times*. April 2, 2016, C1

34. Molly Ball, "Is the Repulican Establishment Giving Up on Ted Cruz?" *The Atlantic*, July 21, 2016.
35. Harry Enten, "America's Distaste for Trump and Clinton is Record-Breaking," *Five Thirty Eight*, May 5, 2016.
36. Scott Clement, "Negative Views of Donald Trump Just Hit a New Campaign High: 7 in 10 Americans," *The Washington Post*, June 15, 2016.
37. David Lauter, "The Least Popular Guy in Politics," *The Los Angeles Times*, April 2, 2016, A1
38. Trip Gabriel, "Policy is not his Point," *The New York Times*, August 5, 2015.
39. Daniel W. Drezner, "The Unique Horror of Donald Trump's Foreign Policy and Why I Signed a Letter Opposing It," *The Washington Post*, March 3, 2016.
40. Lily Rothman, "Donald Trump's 'America First' Policy," *Time*, March 28, 2016.
41. Peter Graff, "Trump's 'America First' Speech Alarms U.S. Allies," *Reuters*, April 29, 2016.
42. Michael Crawley, "Foreign Policy Experts Fret Over Trump's America First Approach," *Politico*, July 20, 2017.
43. Matt Flegenheimer and Maggie Haberman, "Donald Trump, Abortion Foe, Eyes 'Punishment' for Women, Then Recants," *The New York Times*, March 30, 2016.
44. Peter Fenn, "Not Qualified to be President," *U.S. News*, May 4, 2016.
45. *National Enquirer* Staff, "Supreme Court Justice Scalia–Murdered by a Hooker," March 4, 2016.
46. Dan Spinelli, "Trump Revives Rumor Linking Cruz's Father to JFK Assassination," *POLITICO*, July 22, 2016
47. The Viewpoint, *The Week*, April 15, 2016, p. 12.
48. Tribune News Services, "Cruz Refuses to be Trump's 'Servile Puppy' After Attacks on His Wife, Father," *Chicago Tribune*, July 21, 2016.
49. Roper Center, "Two Thumbs Down: 2016 Presidential Candidates Favorability," April 2016.
50. Tribune News Services, "Cruz Refuses to be Trump's 'Servile Puppy' After Attacks on His Wife, Father"
51. Ibid.

52. Donovan Slack, "Trump Bizzarely Links Cruz's Father to JFK Assassination; Cruz Goes Ballistic," *USA Today*, May 3, 2016.
53. "Trump and Clinton Finish with Historically Poor Images," *Gallup Poll*, November 8, 2016.
54. Jia Tolentino, "Trump and the Truth: The 'Mexican Judge,'" *The New Yorker*, September 20, 2016.
55. Heather Caygle, "Ryan: Trump's Comments Textbook Definition of Racism," *Politico*, June 7, 2016.
56. Nick Gass, "Trump Boosted, Clinton Hurt by Primary Media Coverage," *POLITICO*, June 14, 2016.
57. David Lauter, "Trump's 'edge' with the Media," *The Los Angeles Times*, June 14, 2016, A6.
58. Janet Hook, Beth Reinhard, Reid J. Epstein, "Orlando Shooting Widens Hillary Clinton, Donald Trump Divide," *Wall Street Journal*, June 13, 2016.
59. Sam Frizell, "Donald Trump Faces Backlash for Tweet About Orlando Shooting," *Time*, June 12, 2016.
60. Jenna Johnson, "Donald Trump Seems to Connect President Obama to Orlando Shooting," *The Washington Post*, June 13, 2016.
61. Dana Milbank, "Trump Exploits Orlando's Tragedy to Smear Muslims and Obama," *The Washington Post*, June 13, 2016.
62. Editorial, *Los Angeles Times*, June 14, 2016, A12.
63. Jonathan Martin and Maggie Haberman, "Corporations Grow Nervous About Participating in Republican Convention," *The New York Times*, March 30, 2016
64. Ibid.
65. Ibid.
66. Ibid.
67. Ibid.
68. Ibid.
69. Ibid.
70. Ibid.
71. Ibid.
72. Ben White, "Wall Street Shuns Trump's Cleveland Convention," *POLITICO*, July 13, 2016.
73. Scott Clement, "Negative Views of Donald Trump just hit a new campaign high: 7 in 10 Americans," *The Washington Post*, June 15, 2016.

74. Eric Lichtblau and Michal D. Shear, "F.B.I. Director Testifies on Clinton Emails to Withering Criticism from G.O.P.," *The New York Times*, July 7, 2016.

75. Shoshana Weissmann, "Gowdy Grills FBI Director Over Hillary Email Investigation," *The Weekly Standard*, July 7, 2016.

76. For the impact of the Trump children in the campaign, see Lizzie Widdicombe, "First Family: The Influence of Ivanka Trump and Jared Kushner," *The New Yorker*, August 22, 2016.

77. Oliver Darcy, "Trump was 'so unsure' About Selecting Pence as VP He Tried to Get Out of it at Midnight," *Business Insider*, July 15, 2016.

78. Ibid.

79. Ibid.

80. Kelly O'Donald, "Trump Wavered on Pence Pick After News Leaked," *CNBC*, July 16, 2016.

81. Philip Bump, "Donald Trump Just Turned a Key Moment Into a Complete Mess (once again)," *The Washington Post*, July 15, 2016.

82. Eric Bradner, Dana Bash, and MJ Lee, "Donald Trump Selects Mike Pence as VP," *CNN*, July 16, 2016.

83. Tessa Berenson, "Donald Trump Introduces Mike Pence as Vice President Pick," *Time*, July 16, 2016.

84. Ibid.

85. Ibid.

86. Noah Bierman, "Ohio Gov. John Kasich is Everywhere (Except the Convention), Condemning Donald Trump (Without Naming Him)," *The Los Angeles Times*, July 21, 2016.

87. Jessica Taylor, "Dumpster Fires, Fishing, and Travel: These Republicans are Sitting Out of the RNC," *NPR*, July 18, 2016.

88. Ibid.

89. Peter Sullivan, "Kasich Defends Decision to Skip Conventions," *The Hill*, July 19, 2016.

90. Collier Meyerson, "So we counted all the women and people of color at the DNC and the RNC... ," Fusion, July 27, 2016, http://fusion.net/story/330193/dnc-rnc-women-people-of-color-numbers/.

91. Ibid.

92. Scott Baio is an American actor who is best known for his role as Chachi Arcola on the sitcom *Happy Days* (1977–1984) and its spin-off *Joanie Loves Chachi* (1982–1983), as well as the title character

on the sitcom *Charles in Charge* (1984–1990). See http://www.imdb. com/name/nm0000281/bio.

93. Ralph Z. Hallow, "RNC Weighs Scrapping Convention Rule Book to Head-Off Anti-Trump Maneuvers," *The Washington Times*, March 16, 2016.

94. Jason Devaney, "NH Ex-Senator Gordon Humphrey: Trump Supports 'Brownshirts,'" *Newsmax*, July 18, 2016.

95. Ibid.

96. Zeke J. Miller and Alex Altman, "Convention Floor Erupts After Never Trump Action Fails," *TIME Magazine*, July 18, 2016.

97. Anita Kelly, "Section of Melania Trump's Monday Speech Mirrors Michelle Obama's in 2008," *NPR*, July 19, 2016.

98. Ibid.

99. James Hohmann, "The Daily 202: Melania's Plagiarized Convention Speech Shows Trump's Campaign is Still Not Ready for Prime Time," *The Washington Post*, July 19, 2016

100. Gina Barreca, "Can't Give Melania Any Credit for Speech," *Hartford Courant*, July 20, 2016.

101. Ibid.

102. Conor Friedersdorf, "Trump Advisors: Hillary Clinton 'Should be Shot in a Firing Squad for Treason,'" *The Atlantic*, August 16, 2016.

103. Mark Z. Barabok and Noah Bierman, "Trump's Populist Promise," *Los Angeles Times*, May 22, 2016, B1.

104. Alex Altman, "Midnight in America: Donald Trump's Gloomy Convention Speech," *Time*, July 21, 2016.

105. Ibid.

106. Ibid.

107. The Editorial Board, "President Trump Fails NATO," *The New York Times*, May 26, 2017.

108. Jordain Carney, "McConnell: Trump's NATO Remarks a 'Rookie Mistake,'" *The Hill*, July 21, 2016.

109. Editorial, "Toxic Politics of 'Lock her up," *Los Angeles Times*, July 21, 2016, A14.

110. Gabriel Debenedetti and Burgess Everett, " Kaine Brings Down the House in Miami," *POLITICO*, July 23, 2016.

111. Michael Crowley, "Trump Urges Russia to Hack Clinton's Email," *POLITICO*, July 27, 2017.

112. Ibid.

113. Ibid.
114. Eliza Collins, "The Trump-Khan Feud: How We Got Here," *USA Today*, August 1, 2016.
115. Ibid.
116. Kristen Hubby, How Many Americans Actually Vote," *The Daily Dot*, December 19, 2016.

CHAPTER 3

THE GENERAL

THE ULTIMATE OUTSIDER
VERSUS THE ULTIMATE INSIDER

Voting for president presents the citizen with a binary choice. With only two "real" candidates remaining, it is an either/or choice. Ideally, we would have two excellent choices, but the choices for this election were more along the lines of which was the lesser of the two evils, or the evil of two lessers.

And remember, it is not one national presidential election, but fifty-plus separate elections, the results of which are funneled into the Electoral College, the real "decider" of a presidential contest. Your vote counts, but probably not the way you think.

The week after the Democratic convention went poorly for Donald Trump. First, Trump picked a very public fight with Khizr and Ghazala Khan, the parents of Humayan Khan, the Army Captain who died in Iraq in 2004 protecting his troops from a suicide bomber. Mr. Khan gave a short presentation at the Democratic Convention and it rubbed Trump the wrong way. Rather than simply express sorrow for their loss and respect for the sacrifice of their son, Trump repeatedly went after the Khans. Apart from the foolishness of attacking a "Gold Star" family, Trump kept going after the Khans day after day, keeping this story—and Trump's very unpresidential response—alive.[1] It made Trump appear mean and unsympathetic.

Some Trump supporters expressed doubts about their commitment to Trump, including Senator John McCain, who Trump declared that "He's not a war hero" because "he was captured. I like people who weren't captured."[2]

Then in an interview with George Stephanopoulos on the ABC News program "This Week," Trump gave a muddled response to questions dealing with Russia's invasion, occupation, and annexation of portions of Crimea, in the Ukraine. Trump seemed not to know that Russia had annexed the Crimea saying, "He's [Putin] not going into Ukraine. Ok, just so you understand." Trump repeated this and offered that as president, he might recognize Russia's claim in Crimea and end sanctions against Russia. Trump insisted Russia was not in Crimea, which led to this exchange:

> Trump: "He's not going into Ukraine, O.K., just so you understand. He's not going to go into Ukraine, all right? You can mark it down. You can take it anywhere you want. "
>
> Stephanopoulos: "Well he's already there, isn't he?"
>
> Trump: "O.K., well he's there in a certain way. But I'm not there. You have Obama there. And frankly, that whole part of the world is a mess under Obama with all the strength that you're talking about and all of the power of NATO and all of this. In the meantime, he's going away. He take —takes Crimea."[3]

In the same week, the *New York Post* blared a headline *Ménage A Trump* and released some very revealing nude photographs of

Trump's third and current wife Melania Trump that were taken before they were married. It is unfair to Mrs. Trump to be treated thus, but this campaign was in the mud from the very beginning.[4]

In yet another Trump kerfuffle, Trump accused the presidential debate committee of favoring Hillary Clinton by scheduling two of the three debates to conflict with the National Football League (NFL) games. Trump went so far to say that the NFL sent him a letter complaining about this scheduling.[5] The only problem was that the debate dates were decided over a year ago, and the NFL never communicated with Trump about the scheduling issue.

Down to Ten: As the conventions ended, it became clear that the 2016 race would boil down to around ten states. The Democrats entered the general election with about 220 secure electoral votes to the Republicans 170. Ten key states would determine the outcome (see table 1). In 2012, President Obama won nine of those ten states. How would Trump turn the tables on the Democrats?

Table 1a. The Ten Key Contested States, 2016.

State	# Electoral Votes	2012 Results	Margin of Difference
Florida	29	Ob: 49.9% - Rom: 49.3%	.6%
Ohio	18	Ob: 50.1% - Rom: 48.2%	1.9%
North Carolina	15	<u>Ob: 48.4% - Rom: 50.6%</u>	2.2%
Virginia	13	Ob: 50.8% - Rom: 47.8%	3%
Colorado	9	Ob: 51.2% - Rom: 46.5%	4.7%
Pennsylvania	20	Ob: 52% - Rom: 46.8%	5.2%

Table 1b. The Ten Key Contested States, 2016 (*Cont'd*).

State	# Electoral Votes	2012 Results	Margin of Difference
Iowa	6	Ob: 52.1% - Rom: 46.5%	5.6%
New Hampshire	4	Ob: 52.2% - Rom: 46.4%	5.8%
Nevada	6	Ob: 52.3% - Rom: 45.7%	6.6%
Wisconsin	10	Ob: 52.8% - Rom: 46.1%	6.7%

The postconvention campaign got off to a very bad start for Trump. His refusal to endorse Republican Speaker of the House Paul Ryan along with his refusal to endorse Senator John McCain in their reelection bids caused an explosion of anger among establishment Republicans. Some jumped ship, others went so far as to announce they would be voting for Clinton. In addition, Trump's inability to move away from the Khan incident left Republicans worried about the political as well as psychological underpinnings of Trump. News reports suggested that Rudy Giuliani and Newt Gingrich were about to stage an intervention with the candidate, while others openly asked if Trump should consider withdrawing from the race. Still other Republicans openly asserted that Trump had a "personality disorder."[6] Things were looking pretty good for Clinton.

On August 3, with the campaign reeling out of control, Chuck Todd on MSNBC reported that the Trump campaign was in "total and complete chaos." From "No Drama Obama" to "All Drama Trump."[7] Could America stand a constant, four-year barrage of Trump's antics?

If Trump created headaches for the Republican establishment, he continued to delight his loyal followers. Trump continued to stoke the fires of anger and resentment. The forces and feelings he ignited burned ferociously as his appeals to what is worst in us struck a deep chord in those who felt victimized and left behind. The forces of modernity and globalization left many anxious and afraid. Trump gave voice, meaning, and direction to their emotions. He channeled their anger at "them," pointing to the "other" as the cause of trouble.[8] And his simplistic solutions (e.g., build a wall) gave sustenance to a hungry crowd.

The Clinton general election campaign alternated between bland and boring. Clinton herself was not an inspiring rhetorician and seemed unable to warm up to her audience or get the audience to warm up to her. To their benefit, the Trump campaign's missteps seemed to attract most media attention, and the Clinton team was able to fly below the radar most of the time. The problem, however, was that Clinton seemed unable to take advantage of the repeated Trump blunders. He sank, but Clinton did not rise.

On August 8, a toned-down Donald Trump delivered a major address outlining his economic policy. It included large tax cuts, the elimination of the inheritance tax, negotiating new trade agreements, reducing regulations on business and Wall Street, but it also called for spending increases on infrastructure, the military, and no cuts in Social Security or Medicare. Almost immediately, mainstream economists blasted Trump as naive and dangerous. Trump's numbers just didn't add up. Cuts in taxes and increases in spending would bankrupt our already-strained treasury, and what increased tax revenue might come from greater business investment paled in comparison to the budget-busting spending Trump was proposing.

If Trump hoped August 8 would boost his position, he was sorely disappointed when fifty prominent senior Republican national security experts, including former cabinet secretaries, signed an open letter announcing they would not be voting for Trump. The letter said that Trump "would be the most reckless president in American history," and that he "lacks the character, values and experience to be president." They further argued that he "would put at risk our country's national security and well-being."[9]

And the defections just kept on coming, with Republican House Members Scott Rigell of Virginia announcing that he would not be voting for his party's nominee, but would instead vote for Libertarian Party candidate Gary Johnson.[10] This was the third Republican House Member to announce they would not vote for Trump (the others were Representative Richard Hanna of New York[11] and Adam Kitzinger of Illinois[12]).

The hemorrhaging of support continued the next day when Republican Senator Susan Collins of Maine announced that she would not be voting for Trump.[13]

In mid-August, Clinton had yet another e-mail crisis. E-mails came to light from Clinton's time as Secretary of State, suggesting that donors to the Clinton Foundation might have been granted favors by Secretary Clinton.[14] But this potentially explosive incident was defused when Trump declared that President Obama and Secretary Clinton were the "founders of ISIS."[15] Trump repeated this charge several times, and even when given a chance to clarify, Trump stuck to his claim that they were the founders of ISIS.[16] This grabbed almost all the headlines, taking away what would have been a very negative spotlight off Clinton. Trump was proving to be beneficial to the Clinton team.

With his poll numbers collapsing rapidly, on August 17 Trump announced yet another major shakeup in his campaign team. Paul Manafort was demoted, and added to the top echelon were Kellyanne Conway (a prominent Republican pollster) as campaign manager and Steve Bannon, head of right wing Breitbart News, as campaign chief executive.[17] This marked the third stage in the evolution (or devolution) of the Trump campaign team (see table 2).

Was this an act of hope or desperation? Campaigns do go through changes. Top personnel come and go. Ronald Reagan fired his campaign chief the day after he lost the New Hampshire primary in 1980, and reignited his campaign. But three major campaign organizational systems—especially with the third stage coming so close to the election—was a sign of how much trouble the campaign was in. Was the problem one of campaign management or of the candidate himself?

Rearranging the deck chairs on the Titanic would not be enough to turn Trump's fortune around. That is where Steve Bannon came in. His approach was a no-holds-barred, go-for-the-jugular attack style. Clinton is rising in the polls? Tear her down.[18] The signs were clear and ugly: a personalized attack campaign was about to get a whole lot uglier.[19]

A few days later, perhaps reading the writing on the wall, Manafort resigned from the Trump campaign. But if the wheels were falling off the Trump bus, why didn't the entire campaign implode? Why was Trump still only 9–10 points behind Clinton?

Table 2. Trump Campaign Management Team.

Stage	Top Team	Task	Approach
1	Cory Lewandowski	Primary	Let Trump Be Trump Appeal to Angry and Disaffected
2	Paul Manafort	Convention Management	Make Trump Grow Up Bring in base of Republican Party
3	Manafort ($\downarrow$), Conway + Bannon ($\uparrow$)	General Election	Let Trump Be Trump Scorched Earth vs. Hillary vs. Being Presidential

On Monday, August 22, Nate Silver's highly respected website FiveThirtyEight, which does not predict percentage or states directly but gives probability outcomes, gave Hillary Clinton an 84.1% of winning the election.[20]

Clinton's e-mail problems just wouldn't go away. In late August, a new set of e-mails from her time as Secretary of State were released. Some revealed that donors to the Clinton Foundation were asking for access to Secretary Clinton. Some of these requests were flatly rejected, but others did seem to "buy access." No quid pro quo seemed to take place, but the "pay-to-play" attitude hounded Clinton for the rest of the campaign.[21]

As the two camps continued to stumble along, one thing became clear: the only person Clinton could beat was Trump, and the only person Trump could beat was Clinton. Trump's initial strategy seemed to hold on and wait for Clinton to set her campaign on fire. And to some, the ongoing e-mail scandal looked like it might just supply the needed kindling. It all seemed a question of not who would win the election, but who would lose it.

As August rolled into September, the race began to tighten. Trump kept hitting Clinton with accusations of hidden mysterious illnesses that disqualified her from office.[22] And, as if on cue, Clinton left the 9/11 memorial service early and was caught on tape stumbling as she got into a car. The campaign then revealed that Clinton was diagnosed a few days earlier with a mild pneumonia.[23] The campaign's lack of transparency—a recurring issue—and the timing of her illness fed perfectly into the Trump narrative of raising questions about her overall ability to serve.

At the same time, Trump was dogged with the blowback from the signature issue that endeared Trump to the reactionary right: The Obama "birther" issue. Trump made a name for himself attacking Obama, claiming he was not born in the United States, and trying to delegitimize the nation's first black president. Pressed to admit his obvious error, Trump instead announced that Hillary Clinton was the one who had raised the birther issue—this was not true— and that it was Trump who put to rest that lie.[24] It was a whopper. There was no way Trump could get away with this: Or was there?

A review of some of Trump's previous comments reveals that Trump was the one championing the birther issue and yet, his supporters were unperturbed—the "Teflon Don" got away with yet another one.

> "Why doesn't he show his birth certificate? There's some-thing on that birth certificate that he doesn't like." (March 23, 2011, *The View*)

"I want him to show his birth certificate!" (March 23, 2011, *The View*)

"He doesn't have a birth certificate, or if he does, there's something on that certificate that is very bad for him." (March 30, 2011, *The Laura Ingraham Show*)

"I have people that have been studying [Obama's birth certificate] and they cannot believe what they're finding." (April 7, 2011, NBC *Today* show)

"If he wasn't born in this country which is a real possibility ... then he has pulled one of the great cons in the history of politics." (April 7, 2011, NBC *Today* show)

"An 'extremely credible source' has called my office and told me that @BarackObama's birth certificate is a fraud." (Aug. 6, 2012, in a tweet more than a year after Obama released his long-form birth certificate)[25]

And then, finally:

"President Barack Obama was born in the United States. Period." Sept. 16, 2016 [26]

In a polarized age, perhaps the two most polarizing figures in American politics secured the nomination of their parties for the presidency. And as expected, they ran a harsh, nasty race. "The nastiest race, even" was how some dubbed it.[27] Hardly.

While the 2016 race certainly was mean-spirited and conducted mostly from the gutter, one would do well to remember that in America, electoral politics has always had its seamy side. The presidential election of 1800 is but one of many examples one could sight. It was the first truly contested election with two rival parties —the Federalists represented by President John Adams and the Jeffersonians—and it got ugly very quickly.

The President of Yale University, the Reverend Timothy Dwight, an Adams supporter, warned from the pulpit at one of his Sunday services:

> If Jefferson is elected, the Bible will be burned, the French "Marseillaise" will be sung in Christian churches, and we may see our wives and daughters the victims of legal prostitution; soberly dishonored; speciously polluted.[28]

Not to be outdone, one of Jefferson's supporters claimed that Adams was "a hideous hermaphrodital character which neither had the force and firmness of a man, nor the gentleness and sensibility of a woman."[29]

THE DEBATES

The first debate on September 26 was a highly anticipated event; both camps knew that a great deal hinged on a good performance. The Trump team tried to build up Clinton as an experienced and adept debater in hopes that public expectations would be raised so high that even a stellar performance might be seen as a disappointment.

The Clinton team had a different problem: which Donald Trump would show up for the debate, the blustering insult-monger, or the more subdued, presidential Trump? Insults won the Republican primary debates, but this was different. Thus, the Clinton team had to prepare two different debate strategies for two different Trumps.

The consensus was that Hillary Clinton clearly got the better of Trump in this first debate.[30] Perhaps not a knockout, but certainly a TKO (technical knockout). On body language and facial expression, Trump looked like a spoiled child, smirking his way from start to finish—not at all presidential. The grown-up versus the spoiled child debate was partly the result of Clinton's preparation and Trump's lack of preparation. And what do you want, a president who wings it or a president who puts in the hard hours of work? Trump clearly was unprepared, and it showed.

Both had a deficit reduction problem to deal with. Clinton's was the trust deficit, Trump's was the loose-cannon deficit. Clinton may not have done much to close her gap, but Trump hurt himself in the debate, often playing into the negative narrative.

There were lots of ups and downs, but clearly, Clinton won on points. Not a slam dunk but a victory nevertheless for Clinton. In this one-on-one, Trump did not have "game."

Question: What is the weirdest day in U.S. presidential campaign history? I'd nominate October 7, 2016, as the winner (or loser, depending on how one sees this). On the afternoon of that day, the *Washington Post* released a video tape of Donald Trump from 2005, in which he described women in words so vulgar and insulting that the words had to be bleeped out by the news reports.[31] This story spread like wildfire, doing damage to the Trump campaign.

Trump was on his way to a film studio where he was to do a guest appearance on a soap opera. He was with Billy Bush of the TV show "Access Hollywood." Here is the transcript:[32]

Donald J. Trump: You know and ...

Unknown: She used to be great. She's still very beautiful.

Trump: I moved on her, actually. You know, she was down in Palm Beach. I moved on her, and I failed. I'll admit it.

Unknown: Whoa.

Trump: I did try and fuck her. She was married.

Unknown: That's huge news.

Trump: No, no, Nancy. No, this was [unintelligible] — and I moved on her very heavily. In fact, I took her out furniture shopping. She wanted to get some furniture. I said, "I'll show you where they have some nice furniture." I took her out furniture — I moved on her like a bitch. But I couldn't get there. And she was married. Then all of a sudden I see her, she's now got the big phony tits and everything. She's totally changed her look.

Billy Bush: Sheesh, your girl's hot as shit. In the purple.

Trump: Whoa! Whoa!

Bush: Yes! The Donald has scored. Whoa, my man!

[Crosstalk]

Trump: Look at you, you are a pussy.

[Crosstalk]

Trump: All right, you and I will walk out.

[Silence]

Trump: Maybe it's a different one.

Bush: It better not be the publicist. No, it's, it's her, it's —

Trump: Yeah, that's her. With the gold. I better use some Tic Tacs just in case I start kissing her. You know, I'm automatically attracted to beautiful — I just start kissing them. It's like a magnet. Just kiss. I don't even wait. And when you're a star, they let you do it. You can do anything.

Bush: Whatever you want.

Trump: Grab 'em by the pussy. You can do anything.

Bush: Uh, yeah, those legs, all I can see is the legs.

Trump: Oh, it looks good.

Bush: Come on shorty.

Trump: Ooh, nice legs, huh?

Bush: Oof, get out of the way, honey. Oh, that's good legs. Go ahead.

Trump: It's always good if you don't fall out of the bus. Like Ford, Gerald Ford, remember?

Bush: Down below, pull the handle.

Trump: Hello, how are you? Hi!

Arianne Zucker: Hi, Mr. Trump. How are you? Pleasure to meet you.

Trump: Nice seeing you. Terrific, terrific. You know Billy Bush?

Bush: Hello, nice to see you. How you doing, Arianne?

Zucker: Doing very well, thank you. Are you ready to be a soap star?

Trump: We're ready, let's go. Make me a soap star.

Bush: How about a little hug for the Donald? He just got off the bus.

Zucker: Would you like a little hug, darling?

Trump: O.K., absolutely. Melania said this was O.K.

Bush: How about a little hug for the Bushy? I just got off the bus.

Zucker: Bushy, Bushy.

Bush: Here we go. Excellent. Well, you've got a nice co-star here.

Zucker: Yes, absolutely.

Trump: Good. After you.

[Break in video]

Trump: Come on, Billy, don't be shy.

Bush: Soon as a beautiful woman shows up, he just, he takes off. This always happens.

Trump: Get over here, Billy.

Zucker: I'm sorry, come here.

Bush: Let the little guy in here, come on.

Zucker: Yeah, let the little guy in. How you feel now? Better? I should actually be in the middle.

Bush: It's hard to walk next to a guy like this.

Zucker: Here, wait, hold on.

Bush: Yeah, you get in the middle, there we go.

Trump: Good, that's better.

Zucker: This is much better. This is —

Trump: That's better.

Zucker: [Sighs]

Bush: Now, if you had to choose honestly between one of us. Me or the Donald?

Trump: I don't know, that's tough competition.

Zucker: That's some pressure right there.

Bush: Seriously, if you had — if you had to take one of us as a date.

Zucker: I have to take the Fifth on that one.

Bush: Really?

Zucker: Yup — I'll take both.

Trump: Which way?

Zucker: Make a right. Here we go. [inaudible]

Bush: Here he goes. I'm gonna leave you here.

Trump: O.K.

Bush: Give me my microphone.

Trump: O.K. Oh, you're finished?

Bush: You're my man, yeah.

Trump: Oh, good.

Bush: I'm gonna go do our show.

Zucker: Oh, you wanna reset? O.K.

Now, I'm no prude, and I've even used some of those words before —when I was fourteen! Grown-ups simply do not say such words... at least not the grown-ups I know. How could the Republicans defend such vile language? How could they vote for someone like this? And what woman would vote for Trump after hearing those insulting words? Almost immediately after release of the Trump tape, key Republicans sought to distance themselves from Trump. Head of the Republican National Committee Reince Priebus issued a statement condemning Trump, adding "no woman should ever be described in these terms or talked about in this manner. Ever."[33]

House Speaker Paul Ryan cancelled an appearance—set for the following day—with Trump.[34] A few hours later, Trump's vice-presidential running mate Mike Pence, saying he was "offended" by Trump's remarks, also cancelled plans for an appearance with Trump.[35] Even wife Melania said her husband's remarks were "unacceptable and offensive."[36] Could Trump stop the bleeding? Was this the end?

Trump released a statement referring to his remarks as "locker room banter" then going on the attack against Bill Clinton, concluding, "I apologize if anyone was offended."[37] "If," *if?* Who would not be offended? And yet, there were still Republicans actually coming to Trump's defense.

Some Republican's tried the "the best defense is a good offense" strategy, ignoring Trump's remarks and instead going on the attack against Bill Clinton and his checkered past. It was a weak defense.[38]

Trump's initial effort to explain away his crude remarks failed, so late on the evening of October 7, shortly after midnight, Trump released a short recorded statement in which he gave a brief apology, and then went on the attack slamming Hillary Clinton and criticizing Bill Clinton.[39]

How could Trump survive this?

But the day got even stranger, as WikiLeaks released what was believed to be transcripts of Clinton's well-paid speeches to Wall Street audiences. During the primaries, as Bernie Sanders rose, he forced Clinton to move left, and one issue on which she moved left was trade and her objection to Trans-Pacific Partnership (TPP). But the released transcripts painted a different picture. She spoke like a free-trade advocate to Wall Street but did a 180-degree swivel when speaking to her party.[40] Her bad news was—to a degree— drowned out by Trump's sex-talk tape, but would the left of her party abandon her given her hypocrisy on the trade issue?

After the Trump sex-talk tape was aired, supporters dropped off the Trump train as roughly one out of three Republican Senators withdrew their support for Trump, and the Republican Speaker of the House said he would no longer defend Trump.[41] There was open discussion of ways to force Trump off the ticket. But Trump was defiant. If he was going down, he was taking everyone with him. He decided to "go nuclear."[42]

The second presidential debate took place on Sunday, October 9. Since the first debate, Hillary Clinton's poll numbers began to rise, and campaign insiders believed that the second debate might be Trump's last chance to make a dent in Clinton's lead. But how would Trump's vulgar references to women, and Clinton's duplicity on trade, impact the debates?

The predebate dramatics alone were worthy of mention as Donald Trump held a press conference featuring several women who claimed that in the 1980s and 90s, Bill Clinton had made inappropriate sexual advances towards them, including one claim of rape.[43]

Designed to throw Clinton off balance by turning the sexual harass-
ment accusation around onto Clinton, this "go low" effort to further
sink the campaign into the gutter may have unnerved Clinton as
her debate performance was not especially strong.

The "X" rated nature of these revelations and campaign schemes
meant that many parents felt they could not allow their children to
watch the unfolding pageant of a presidential election. What was to
be a high point of American politics descended into a low and dirty
effort to assail character and personally damage the opposition.

The debate itself was riveting, yet unsatisfying. Trump was in
full attack mode, launching into a series of assaults on Clinton and
her husband. He called Clinton "the devil," repeatedly interrupted
her, and hovered over her in what some saw as a menacing or
threatening manner.[44] Trump announced that if he became president
he would appoint a special prosecutor to go after Clinton adding
that if he were President "you'd be in jail," adding later, "she has
tremendous hate in her heart."[45]

Clinton decided not to rise to the bait. While she was critical
of Trump, she did not match Trump's seething anger in kind.
This left some to criticize her as "tepid" in response to Trump's
forceful performance, but most commentators believed that her
calm demeanor was a striking contrast to Trump's anger.[46]

Trump succeeded in stopping some of the bleeding of his
campaign, but throwing red meat to his base did nothing to expand
it—an important step if he hoped to win in November.

The consensus was that while Trump was on the offensive in
debate two, he did little to help himself, and that Clinton's more
subdued style gave her the victory. Polls reflected this as Trump
slipped 3 to 4 points and Clinton gained ground. [47]

Trump's response? An all-out, no holds barred attack. It was a scorched earth approach, with Trump at war not only with the Clintons, but also with the Republican Party as well. It was as if Trump were running for President of Alt Nation and not the United States. And he only dug himself deeper into a hole. Rather than change course and abandon a failing approach, Trump charged wildly ahead.

A "leader" telling a political opponent that if he were president, "you'd be in jail" is the stuff of Tin-Pot dictatorship and is a basic and fundamental threat to the rule of law and democratic values. And afterwards, when the dust settled, did Trump back down from this statement? No, he kept repeating it to the cheers of his adoring followers. We were coming close to a danger zone in our country.

THE GREAT FLIP-FLOP

For a year, Donald Trump talked like a man running for President of Fox News. His singular issue, immigration, got him national attention and catapulted him to the early lead in the GOP primaries. He promised to round up and deport all of the nearly 11 million people who were undocumented in the United States, ship them back to their countries of origin, build a wall, and have Mexico pay for it.[48] Supporters flocked to Trump and his draconian dystopian vision. He appealed to and brought out the worst in his party. But it worked!

In the beginning of the general election Trump doubled down, emphasizing his harsh approach to immigrants. The only problem was that what got him there might not get him to the White House. As he fell further and further behind Clinton it became clear that Trump had to change his message. But how could he? Trump was so identified with his deportation and the "build a wall" positions that to back away would be startling.

A flip-flop of nuclear proportions ... could he? Should he? Would he? No way.

After repeating over and over again during the primaries that he would round up and deport 11 million illegal immigrants, the Donald did a flip, then a flop. Trump betrayed the very issue commitment on which his candidacy was based from day one. He backed off virtually every element of his deportation promises (the exception being that he would still deport "criminals").[49] Could his supporters stomach such a reversal (a betrayal)? Trump went from the Terminator to Amnesty-lite. With principles grounded in Jell-O, Trump appeared to be just another politician who would say and do anything to get elected.

Oh, and his primary race promise to "ban all Muslims"? That too got jettisoned.[50] Mr. Outsider had morphed into Mr. Politician.

As August rolled around into September, Clinton continued to hold a lead over Trump in the polls. But Trump was within striking distance. His campaign team expressed unbridled optimism due to their belief that there were scores of "underground Trump voters": people too ashamed to admit publicly that they were for Trump, who would—come November 8—go to the polls liberated in the secrecy of the voting booth and go for Trump. Apart from the obvious question of just how bad could Trump be that his supporters had to hide their preference, was the question: *was there really an army of secret, underground Trump voters?*

The Constitution does not guarantee you the right to vote. Such matters are left to the states, which is why although we have but one presidential election, we have over fifty different sets of rules for how a president is selected in each state, and why voting rights vary from state to state.

In the past seven years, twenty-two states have passed laws restricting the right to vote. Yes, I know, we should be encouraging citizens to participate, but for narrow political gain, 44% of our states are trying to shrink the voting populations. This may be done in a variety of ways: cutting back on early voting, eliminating election-day registration, disenfranchising ex-felons, and the most popular of them all—requiring a higher proof of registration and citizenship—requiring a government-issued ID and photo. This of course means that many of the younger voters, minorities, and the elderly (the groups least likely to possess such forms of identification) may be disenfranchised.[51] And, who is to stop the states from such a blatant thwarting of the democratic process? As Ari Berman notes:

> In the past, the federal government serves as a check against such effort. But in 2013, the Supreme Court invalidated a key section of the 1965 Voting Rights Act, ruling that states with the worst histories of voting discrimination no longer need to have changes to their voting systems approved by the federal government. As a result, 2016 is the first presidential election in 50 years during which citizens won't have the full protections of the Voting Rights Act.[52]

People just didn't trust Hillary Clinton, so when in late August, questions were raised about donors to the Clinton Foundation getting special access to Clinton while she served as secretary of state, people just assumed it was a "pay-to-play" scheme. While no evidence of any quid pro quo deal was uncovered, the appearances were damning. For Clinton, optics mattered as going into any situation, Clinton faced a trust deficit that made accusations—even if untrue—stick.

On the last day of August, Donald Trump took a trip. He went to Mexico City where he held a private meeting with Mexico's President Enrique Pena Nieto. Among the topics discussed *may have* been Trump's controversial "we will build a wall, and Mexico will pay for it" refrain so often shouted to enthusiastic audiences at numerous Trump rallies. *May have* are the key words here.

Following the meeting, Trump said they had not discussed who would pay for the wall, but the Mexican president (@EPN) tweeted on August 31 that "Al inicio de la conversación con Donald Trump dejé claro que México no pagará por el muro," stating that he had said at the beginning of their conversation that Mexico would not be paying for the wall.[53] Wherein lies the truth? But this appearance—a president and Trump standing side by side made Trump seem more presidential.

That evening, in a speech in Phoenix, Arizona, Trump went all in on his anti-immigrant, pro-wall, "Mexico will pay" stance. In a speech Trump displayed his Dr. Jekyll side after the morning Mister Hyde. The speech was harsh, at times nasty and mean-spirited, and all about blaming immigrants for the nation's problems.[54] The old Trump was back!

Trump or Clinton? Clinton or Trump? As the campaign progressed through the fall, voters became more disillusioned by the choices. Popular memes circulated such as "I'm not crazy about Hillary, but I'm not crazy!" and "This is the Henry Youngman (a Borscht Belt comedian from your parents' era) election," in honor of Youngman's signature joke: Q: How's your wife? A: Compared to what?" How is your candidate? Compared to what? This seeemed less like a presidential election and more of a TV reality show that was all about who could trash whom the most.

As the final debate drew near, Trump went on a daily Twitter rant railing against the media,[55] Clinton,[56] fellow Republicans,[57] and even "Saturday Night Live."[58] They were all out to get him, and they were rigging the election. Trump would rant and rave about how if he loses, it will be because the election was stolen.[59] Day after day, Trump would inflame attendees at his rallies with these charges and call on them to monitor voting locations.[60]

Despite Trump's over-the-top charges, or perhaps because of

them, he continued to draw large and enthusiastic crowds at his rallies. The problem—at least electorally—was that Trump's crowds were largely drawn from white, older, and less educated parts of the population. How could this add up to an electoral majority? Trump was strongly supported by his followers, but votes from this group alone—especially with the gender gap widening—might not give Trump a victory.

Clinton had her own problems. WikiLeaks kept releasing Russian-hacked emails stolen from Clinton staffers, some of which caused embarrassment.[61] But the real impact was not the content of the e-mails, but the constant drip, drip, drip of releasing some on Monday, more on Wednesday, and even more and more each day. The seemingly continual releases fed into the Trump-driven narrative that Clinton could not be trusted and had something to hide.

As Trump's poll numbers languished in the low 40% range, and still reeling from the Access Hollywood sex-talk tape, Trump shifted gears and went on the attack against not only Hillary Clinton and her husband Bill (for his sexual escapades),[62] but also the media (who were out to get him),[63] the polls (which were crooked),[64] Carlos Slim (the richest man in Mexico who was part owner of the *New York Times*),[65] the Republican establishment (especially House Speaker Paul Ryan for being disloyal),[66] and international bankers[67] (whom Clinton was directing against Trump). Trump's civil war with his own party indicated the deep rift between the party mainstream and the populist, insurgent right.[68]

The third and final debate took place on October 19 in Las Vegas, Nevada. Trump needed a knockout, Clinton needed no more than to survive the evening unbloodied. As it turned out, the debate was largely underwhelming, except for one key Trump answer.

Moderator Chris Wallace of Fox News asked Trump if—in light of his frequent claims the election was rigged—he would accept the legitimacy of the outcome of the election. Trump's response caused a ruckus:

> Wallace: Mr. Trump, I want to ask you about one last question in this topic. You have been warning at rallies recently that this election is rigged and that Hillary Clinton is in the process of trying to steal it from you.
>
> Your running mate, Governor Pence, pledged on Sunday that he and you - his words - "will absolutely accept the result of this election." Today, your daughter, Ivanka, said the same thing. I want to ask you here on the state tonight: Do you make the same commitment that you will absolutely - sir, that you will absolutely accept the result of this election?
>
> Trump: I will look at it at the time. I'm not looking at anything now. I'll look at it at the time.
>
> What I've seen - what I've seen is so bad. First of all, the media is so dishonest and so corrupt, and the pile-on is so amazing. *The New York Times* actually wrote an article about it, but they don't even care. It's so dishonest. And they poisoned the mind of the voters.
>
> But unfortunately for them, I think the voters are seeing through it. I think they're going to see through it. We'll find out on November 8th. But I think they're going to see through it.
>
> Wallace: But, sir, there's...
>
> Trump: If you look - excuse me, Chris - if you look at your voter rolls, you will see millions of people that are registered to vote - millions, this isn't coming from me - this is coming from Pew Report and other places - millions of people that are registered to vote that shouldn't be registered to vote.

So let me just give you one other thing. So I talk about the corrupt media. I talk about the millions of people - tell you one other thing. She shouldn't be allowed to run. It's crooked - she's - she's guilty of a very, very serious crime. She should not be allowed to run

And just in that respect, I say it's rigged, because she should never ...

Wallace: But...

Trump: Chris, she should never have been allowed to run for the presidency based on what she did with emails and so many other things.

Wallace: But, sir, there is tradition in this country - in fact, one of the prides of this country - is the peaceful transition of power and that no matter how hard-fought a campaign is, that at the end of the campaign that the loser concedes to the winner. Not saying that you're necessarily going to be the loser or the winner, but that the lose conceded to the winner and that the country comes together in part for the good of the country. Are you saying you're not prepared not to commit to that principle?

Trump: What I'm saying is that I will tell you at the time. I'll keep you in suspense. OK?

Clinton: Well, Chris, let me respond to that, because that's horrifying. You know, every time Donald thinks things are not going in his direction; he claims whatever it is, is rigged against him.

The FBI conducted a year-long investigation into my emails. They concluded there was no case; he said the FBI was rigged. He lost the Wisconsin primary. He said the Republican primary was rigged against him. Then Trump University gets sued for fraud and racketeering; he claims the court system and the federal judge is rigged against him. There was even a time when he didn't get an Emmy for his TV program three years in a row and he started tweeting that the Emmys were rigged against him.

Trump: Should have gotten it.

[Laughter]

Clinton: This is - this is his mindset. This is how Donald thinks, and it's funny, but it's also really troubling.

Wallace: OK.

Clinton: So that is not the way our democracy works. We've been around for 240 years. We've had free and fair elections. We've accepted the outcomes when we may not have liked them. And that is what must be expected of anyone standing on a debate stage during a general election. You know, President Obama said the other day when you're whining before the game is even finished

[Applause]

Wallace: Hold on. Hold on, folks. Hold on, folks.

Clinton: ...it just shows you're not up to doing the job. And let's - you know, let's be clear about what he is saying and what that means. He is denigrating - he's talking down our democracy. And I, for one, am appalled that somebody who is the nominee of one of our two major parties would take that kind of position.

Trump: It think what the FBI did and what the Department of Justice did, including meeting with her husband, the attorney general, in the back of an airplane on the tarmac in Arizona, I think it's disgraceful. I think it's a disgrace.

Wallace: All right.

Trump: I think we've never had a situation so bad in this country.

[Applause][69]

Chris Wallace's question was easy, so easy in fact that there was only one answer to the question: YES. But Trump could not hold back. He just could not maintain his presidential persona. From there, everything went downhill.

The headline from the third debate was easy: Trump Refuses to Say he Will Accept Outcome of Election. He was almost universally panned. A debate that started off a draw quickly degenerated into a Clinton victory, and it was Donald Trump who handed Clinton that victory.

The other "interesting" jab took place when Clinton challenged the experience of Trump noting that: "And on the day when I was in the situation room, monitoring the raid that brought Osama bin Laden to justice, he was hosting the 'Celebrity Apprentice.'"[70]

The consensus was that Clinton won the third debate, giving her three wins in three debates. Twenty days left. Could Trump turn things around?

Trump's debate performance played well with his base, but his base was only about 35% of voters. They were already going to vote for Trump, so why keep feeding them red meat at the expense of alienating undecided voters? It seemed to make no sense.

The 2016 election went from being a "change election" (which favored Trump) to a "temperament" election (which favored Clinton). Trump increasingly seemed on the outside looking in.

As the date of the vote approached, most Americans just did not see Trump as presidential.[71]

By mid-day of October 20, Trump did a bit of mea culpa by announcing that he would respect the will of the people "if I win," and added that he intended to accept the outcome of the election. He added "Of course, I would accept a clean election result, but I would also reserve my right to contest or file a legal challenge in the case of a questionable result." Trump concluded that, "and always, I will follow and abide by all of the rules and traditions of all of the many candidates who have come before me. Always."[72] Not quite the full-throated reassurance most had hoped for. Did Trump clear up or further muddy the water?

Down-ticket Republicans—those running for the House and Senate—feared that Trump would take them down with him in defeat. And while it was a legitimate concern, some polling suggested that Republican House and Senate candidates were running ahead of Trump in their states and districts. The Democrats, however, saw the Trump collapse as an opportunity to win majority status in the Senate (where they needed to switch four states) and even (perhaps) in the House (where they needed over thirty seats).

As October drifted into November, it seemed that the race was over. Clinton's focused, disciplined campaign had won out over Trump's flamboyant glitz. In the end, Clinton's experience proved one of the key differences as Trump's mistake-prone campaign—the result of Trump's inexperience and temperament—self-destructed, and there was really no one to blame but Trump himself.

While Clinton ran a lackluster campaign, Trump ran a wild and wacky circus of a political campaign. It was more show business than politics. In the long haul of a campaign season, many began to tire of Trump's show.

After spending ten months discussing, celebrating, and relying on polls that indicated he was ahead in the primaries, all of a sudden in mid-October, Trump said, "I don't believe the polls."[73] Two things were at work here: 1) after rising to a virtual tie with Clinton in the polls, by October the polls signaled roughly a seven-percent lead for Clinton; and 2) his own campaign's internal polls indicated he was about to lose the election.

How did Trump respond? Trump charged that the election was rigged, fixed, corrupt,[74] and that all the pollsters, election officials, international bankers, and others like them had "stolen America's sovereignty."[75] At a news conference held in the White House Rose Garden on October 18, President Barack Obama openly ridiculed Trump, recommending that the Republican presidential nominee "stop whining." The president continued," I have never seen in my lifetime, or in modern political history, any presidential candidate trying to discredit the elections and the election process before votes have even taken place." Obama went on to express doubt at Trump's leadership and toughness to be president.[76]

But Trump persisted; at a rally in Colorado Springs, Colorado, on October 18, he declared that "Voter fraud is all too common, and then they criticize us for saying that. But take a look at Philadelphia, what's been going on, take a look at Chicago, take a look at St. Louis. Take a look at some of these cities, where you see things happening that are horrendous. And if you talk about it, they say bad things about you, they call you a racist."[77]

Increasingly it became clear that there were two Donald Trumps, as well as two Trump campaigns. The first was the Trump of the Kellyanne Conway side of the campaign which appeared to exhort Trump to act presidential, stick to the issues, and not engage in any rants or late-night tweets, or act on any personal vendetta— keep it clean, keep it political, keep it focused. That Trump closed the gap on Clinton.

But the other Trump, the Trump from what seemed to be the Steve Bannon campaign team, kept surfacing. It was also this Trump who lost considerable ground to Clinton. Trump was at his best when he was the Kellyanne Conway campaign Trump. For the last two weeks of the campaign, this was the Trump who took center stage.

Meanwhile, Clinton's e-mail issues kept cropping up. Every few days WikiLeaks would release a batch of new stolen e-mails. The U.S. federal government determined that these e-mails were hacked with the cooperation of the Russian government. To add to the already-bizarre nature of the 2016 race, now the Russians were busy trying to influence the election outcome.[78] Earlier in the campaign, Donald Trump openly encouraged the Russians to release the stolen emails, and it appeared that the Putin government was more than happy to do so,[79] adding more controversy to the already-mystifying bromance between Trump and Putin.

Thankfully, for the Clinton camp, the e-mails did not reveal any smoking gun. What they revealed is what was already widely known: that Hillary Clinton was an extremely "political" politician.

POLICY OR PERSONALITY?

2016 was more about personality than policy, posturing than positions. On the economy, for example, Trump's proposals received little attention. It wasn't a plan he was selling, it was himself. Trump kept repeating that the economy was "a mess" and "a disaster." His solution? During the campaign Trump promised to balance the budget by getting rid of "tremendous waste, fraud, and abuse" (an old Republican bromide that would not come close to eliminating the deficit), but to also boost spending on infrastructure projects, protect Social Security and Medicare, while also providing a multi-trillion dollar tax cut.[80] We tried this in the 1980s under Ronald Reagan and in those eight years, the United States went from being

the world's largest creditor nation to being the world's largest
debtor nation.[81]

LOOKING PRESIDENTIAL FOR A TIME

Kellyanne Conway, Trump's third campaign manager, saw her
job as getting Trump to shift from primary to general campaign
mode. That meant acting more presidential. Corey Lewandowski,
Trump's first campaign manager, was supposed to let Trump be
Trump, fire up the base, debase all opponents, and catch everyone
else by surprise.[82] That primary campaign strategy won Trump the
nomination. But fearing that party insiders might try to rob him
of the nomination, Trump fired Lewandowski and hired long-time
Republican insider Paul Manafort to manage the convention and
secure the delegates. Having done that, Trump's shift to the general
election seemed to require the services of a more temperate voice,
and Conway was hired to soften the harsh edges of the candidate.[83]
For a brief time it worked, and Trump closed the gap with Hillary
Clinton, but it wasn't long before the blistering, bombastic Trump
reemerged in all-out attack mode. This led to a drop in the polls.

Was keeping Trump out of attack mode ever a viable option?
Long-time friend of Trump's and former Speaker of the House Newt
Gingrich did not think so:

> That's not going to happen, because he's a seventy-year-old
> adult billionaire who has been on a top rated TV show, had
> the No.1 book in the country, beat sixteen people, got the
> record number of votes as the nominee. He actually think
> he knows something." Gingrich went on, "Her view is that
> she needs to intuit what he's good at and what he's bad at,
> and how to deal with them.[84]

DUSTUP AT THE AL SMITH DINNER

Every presidential election season, the candidates of the two major parties drop everything and go to New York City to attend and speak at the Alfred E. Smith Memorial Foundation Dinner. This quadrennial campaign ritual is a time when the two rivals can make fun of themselves, and take a few good natured jabs at their opponents—all in good fun, and all for a good cause: To fund Catholic Charities.

Alfred E. "Al" Smith (1873–1944) served as governor of New York, and was the Democratic candidate for president in 1928. He was the first Catholic nominated for president by a major party, and lost the election to Herbert Hoover by a wide margin. Since 1960, the dinner held in his name and hosted by the Catholic Church, has been used to bring the two presidential opponents together for an evening of good natured ribbing.

It should come as no surprise that the 2016 dinner was different. Donald Trump was the first speaker of the evening. He got off a few good lines, such as his attack on the media, charging them with bias saying, "You want the proof? Michelle Obama gives a speech, and everyone loves it. My wife, Melania, gives the exact same speech and people get on her case."

That was the highlight. But most of Trump's jabs sounded snarky and mean-spirited, repeating his "so corrupt" line from his campaign rallies. The performance was described by the *New York Times* as follows:

> Breaking with decades of tradition at the gathering once he took the microphone, Mr. Trump set off on a blistering, grievance-filled performance that translated poorly to the staid setting, stunning many of the well-heeled guests who had filed into the Waldorf Astoria hotel for an uncommon spectacle: an attempted detente in a campaign so caustic that

the candidates, less than 24 hours earlier, declined to shake hands on a debate stage. Relations did not much improve.[85]

Perhaps Trump's lowest blow came when he said, "Here she is tonight, in public pretending not to hate Catholics." A much-deserved round of boos directed at Trump followed.

There were jeers and boos directed at Trump; it was the first time in the history of the dinner that a candidate was booed. The *New York Times* also noted:

> By then, he had decisively lost the room. Those on the dais with him seemed to almost writhe away from him at points - brows furrowing, smiles turning to grimaces. One man beside Mr. Trump became a viral sensation on social media, his face frozen and eye bulged by a quip gone awry.[86]

Clinton, for her part, performed credibly. But Trump was—as usual—the story of the evening. Love him or hate him, he was like a media magnet, drawing all attention to himself. Trump fit the description Theodore Roosevelt's daughter had of her father's hunger for attention: "My father," she said, "always wanted to be the corpse at every funeral, the bride at every wedding, and the baby at every christening." [87]

As the polls continued to show a gap favoring Clinton, Trump pressed his "it's rigged" line, arguing that the media was lying about his poll numbers, and the fix was in for the election. And as an eleventh woman came forward claiming that Trump had sexually assaulted her, Trump went off message, announcing that after the election, every one of those women would be sued.

And while Clinton held a lead, the constant drip of her e-mails (by Russia) forced the Clinton team into a defensive posture.[88] The leaked e-mails revealed were highly political—something that many would see as an asset in a politician—but there were no "smoking guns," at least not yet.

Donald Trump's media savvy was evident when two weeks prior to the election, it was announced that Trump was unveiling a new nightly news program, *Trump Tower Live*, to be broadcast via Facebook. As with his creative use of Twitter, Trump again demonstrated his ability to attract attention (and free media) and become the story. But the program had a very short shelf life.

October 25th should have been a good day for Donald Trump. Reports were released in which it was estimated that the premiums for Obamacare would go up on average 25%. This played right into the Trump wheelhouse. But on the same day, Colin Powell endorsed Clinton and William Weld, the Libertarian Party vice presidential candidate, told his supporters not to waste a vote on his team, and that it was so important to stop Trump that he all but publicly endorsed Clinton.

Trump's manner, off-putting to most, was a part of his persona. He was not politically correct; he was a "man's man." Yet this toughness masked hostility to women and self-doubts. He had too much to prove, too fragile an ego to let his guard down. He always had to prove himself. And such uber manliness had and has consequences. Donald Trump just couldn't accept defeat; it undermined the fragile manly persona he tried so hard to create. And this manifested itself in his threats not to accept the results of the election.

In a late October Suffolk University/USA Today poll, 43% of Trump supporters said they would not accept a Clinton victory as legitimate, with only 35% saying they would accept her victory. It is one thing to attempt to govern after a close election, but when over four in ten people who voted against you refuse to accept that you are the legitimately elected president.[89]

THE COMEY FIRESTORM

Firestorm; a storm of fire, a conflagration of such intensity that it creates its own wind system. And that is what FBI Director James Comey created in the final days of the 2016 presidential race.

On October 29, Comey dropped a bombshell on the Clinton campaign: from a separate investigation not related to Hillary Clinton (one dealing with the strange "sext" case against former House member Anthony Weiner, then married to top Clinton aide Huma Abedin) new e-mails had been discovered, and that the FBI would be reviewing these e-mails to see if they pertained to the Clinton case.

Coming so close to the election, fitting into the Trump "crooked Hillary" narrative, and building upon the already-low level of trust the public had in Clinton, this announcement proved devastating to Clinton. It threw a monkey wrench into the race that opened a door for Trump to potentially march into the White House. A close race just got a whole lot closer.

THE RUSSIANS ARE COMING, THE RUSSIANS ARE COMING

The Clinton e-mail fallout seemed a story without an ending. On and on, every week, more WikiLeaks releases, more questions raised, but few answered. That the Russian government was deemed by seventeen U.S. federal agencies to have hacked the Democrat's e-mails and sent them to WikiLeaks for release was lost amid all the allegations, accusations, FBI on-again, off-again investigations, and the frenetic activities of final-week campaigning. Several Russian officials admitted they had had contacts with a member of the Trump campaign. All of this should not distract us from one essential truth:

the Russian government was meddling in a U.S. election in favor of the Trump campaign.

The steady release of the e-mails was clearly designed to influence the outcome of the election, and Trump was the beneficiary. Where was the public outrage? Where was the FBI?

There is an old saying "leave well enough alone." The flip side of that saying is also useful: leave bad enough alone, or, when in a hole, don't dig yourself deeper into that hole. This is precisely what the FBI did just days after their kerfuffle over Hillary Clinton's (yet-again) e-mails.

On October 31, the FBI handed Donald Trump another plum, releasing 129 pages of documents relating to Bill Clinton's 2001 pardon of fugitive Marc Rich. At the time, the pardon proved an embarrassment for Clinton as Rich's wife had donated considerable money to the Bill Clinton Library Foundation. A president's power to pardon is absolute and unchecked. However, the appearance of a quid pro quo cast the Clintons in an unflattering light. Democrats were quick to pounce on the timing of the FBI release, especially coming on the heels of the Hillary Clinton e-mail announcement the FBI had made a few days earlier, and coming a week before the day of the election.

On Wednesday, six days before the election, the polls were beginning to show Trump taking the lead in several battleground states. For the past two weeks, Trump had been disciplined, stayed on message, and Clinton was hit by a one-two punch from the FBI. Clinton's once-safe lead was in jeopardy. Would there be any more bombshells? Any more FBI announcements? Could Trump stay on message?

In the final days, the election had so tightened up that there was talk of a possible 268 to 268 Electoral College tie, putting the choice for the next president to the Republican-controlled House of Representatives. Even with a winner chosen on November 8, the margin of victory could be so tight that the very legitimacy of the victor might be in doubt.

In reviewing the attempts by the Russian government to undermine the U.S. presidential election, Brian Bennett of *The Los Angeles Time* wrote:

> Russia's attempts to interfere with Hillary Clinton's campaign are not in doubt, according to U.S. officials. They appear to be driven in part by a personal animus against the former secretary of State, officials say, as well as an effort to raise doubts about the validity of U.S. democracy and leadership around the globe.

> On Oct. 7, the Department of Homeland Security and the U.S. Intelligence Community - which comprises the nation's 16 intelligence agencies - said they were confident that Russia's government was responsible for stealing and leaking tens of thousands of emails from accounts used by Democratic National Committee staffers and from the private account of John Podesta, chairman of Clinton's campaign.[90]

RIGGED

Fixing, or rigging a presidential election is, to say the least, exceedingly difficult. But this is precisely what Donald Trump had been saying in the final weeks of the campaign. A cabal of Democrats, the Obamas, the news media, powerful international bankers were all aligned against Trump and orchestrating a rigged electoral victory for Hillary Clinton.

It is easy to dismiss such conspiracy theories as promoted only by those at the fringes, people who wear tinfoil hats. But in 2016, one of the major party candidates was in full-blown conspiracy mode, setting himself up for possible martyrdom "if" the count went against him.[91]

People who believe in conspiracy theories are generally the less educated, with lower incomes, and less trusting of people in general, who seek certainty in their lives and are uncomfortable with complexity.[92]

Rather than showering praise of the American system of separation of powers, rule of law, and checks and balances, Trump praises strong unilateral powers and praises strongmen like Vladimir Putin of Russia.[93] He has publicly threatened that if he is president, he intends to take putative actions against the Richetts family (owners of the Chicago Cubs) because they opposed him in the primaries saying, "Believe me, if I become president, boy do they have problems."[94] He called for the investigation of a federal judge (Curiel) who ruled against him in a case, adding that, "What Judge Curiel is doing is a total disgrace."[95] When told that his plan to kill the families of suspected terrorists was illegal, Trump said, "They're (the U.S. military) not going to refuse me. If I say do it, they're going to do it."[96] And of course he had already called for the prosecution of his opponent, Hillary Clinton, declared her guilty, and assured his cheering audience that if he is elected she will be "in jail."[97]

Things became even crazier when Trump and his supporters began threatening to impeach Hillary Clinton even before the election had taken place. As *The New York Times* editorialized:

> Donald Trump and other embattled Republican candidates are resorting to a particularly bizarre and dangerous tactic in the closing days of the campaign - warning that they may well seek to impeach Hillary Clinton if she wins, or, short of that, tie her up with endless investigations and other delaying tactics.

Trump surrogate Rudy Giuliani went so far as to tell an Iowa audience, "I guarantee you in one year she'll be impeached and indicted."[98]

Sunday afternoon, two days before the election, and FBI Director James Comey released a letter announcing that, after going through the newly discovered batch of emails, the FBI found nothing to charge Clinton with.[99] All that smoke and no fire. But the damage had been done. How much we would find out in two days.

The genie was out of the bottle. Never before had the FBI so deeply intruded in the electoral process as it had done in 2016. Clinton's popularity and support dropped, and her lead evaporated. In a race so seemingly close, how much would Clinton suffer electorally? And what impact would this have on Democrats in down-ballot races? Thirty-nine million (early) votes had already been cast by the time Comey cleared Clinton.

In the waning days of the presidential campaign, candidates usually convey an uplifting, hopeful message, designed to stir and inspire voters. Not in 2016. Both Clinton and Trump hit each other with a series of negative ads designed to crush their opponents, not lift the spirits of their followers. Trump's commercials were especially dark, suggesting that a huge international conspiracy was afoot against him, with international financiers waging war against Trump.[100] This paranoia fed the Trump partisans, but could it sway undecided voters?

Both campaigns attempted an unusual eleventh-hour effort to sway those few voters still undecided: they ran a series of two-minute campaign commercials. These longer commercials ran at prime-time on such Sunday and Monday programs as *The Voice* and Sunday and Monday night football. Trump's commercials were especially dark, perhaps reflecting the expected results of the November 8 election.

NOTES

1. Alexander Burns, "Ignoring Advice, Donald Trump Presses Attack on Khan Family and G.O.P. Leaders," *The New York Times*, August 2, 2016.
2. Ben Schreckinger, "Trump attacks McCain: 'I like people who weren't captured'," *POLITICO*, July 18, 2015, http://www.politico.com/story/2015/07/trump-attacks-mccain-i-like-people-who-werent-captured-120317.
3. Eric Bradner and David Wright, "Trump Says Putin is 'Not Going to Go in Ukraine' Despite Crimea," *CNN*, August 1, 2016.
4. Isabel Vincent, "Melania Trump's girl-on-girl photos from racy shoot revealed," *New York Post*, August 1, 2016, http://nypost.com/2016/08/01/melania-trumps-girl-on-girl-photos-from-racy-shoot-revealed/.
5. Nick Eilerson and Cindy Boren, "NFL Refutes Trump Claim that it Sent Him a Letter Bashing Debate Schedule," *The Washington Post*, July 31, 2016.
6. Dan P. McAdams, "The Mind of Donald Trump," *The Atlantic*, June 20, 2016.
7. Media Matters Staff, "MSNBC's Chuck Todd Details 'The Unraveling' of Trump's Campaign in Last 36 Hours," *Media Matters for America*, August 3, 2016.
8. Susan Page and Brad Heath, "How Anti-Establishment Outsider Donald Trump was Elected," *USA Today*, November 9, 2016.
9. Eric Bradner, Elise Labott, and Dana Bash, "50 GOP National Secuirty Experts Oppose Trump," *CNN*, August 8, 2016.
10. David A. Graham, "Which Republicans are Against Trump?" *The Atlantic*, November 6, 2016.
11. Ibid.
12. Ibid.
13. Ibid.
14. Rosalind S. Helderman, "Hacked Emails Show Extent of Foreign Government Donations to Clinton Foundation," *The Washington Post*, October 16, 2016.

15. Tal Kopan, "Donald Trump Tries to Walk Back Claim Obama Founded ISIS: 'Sarcasm,'" *CNN*, August 12, 2016.

16. Tal Kopan, "Donald Trump I meant that Obama Founded ISIS, Literally," *CNN*, August 12, 2016.

17. Distancing Manafort from Trump became necessary as news stories reported that Manafort was under investigation for his ties to Russian-backed politicians in the Ukraine. Gabrielle Levy, "Paul Manafort Denies New Allegations of Trump-Russia Connection," *US News*, March 22, 2017.

18. Miles Mogulescu, "Don't Underestimate How Much Steve Bannon Can Damage Hillary Clinton," *Huffington Post*, August 26, 2016.

19. Although the Trump campaign downplayed the increased role of disgraced former Fox News head Roger Ailes in his informal advisory role to Trump, adding Ailes to the advisory team further pushed the candidate into attack mode. Strategy and tone took an abrupt shift, as the brawling, pick-a-fight every day Trump of the early primary season was about to be revived.

20. Harry Entin, "Clinton's Post-Convention Bump is Showing No Signs of Fading," *FiveThirtyEight*, August 7, 2016.

21. Rosalind S. Helderman and Tom Hamburger, "Foreign Governments Gave Millions to Foundation While Clinton was at State Department," *The Washington Post*, February 25, 2015.

22. Jonathan Easley, "Trump's Spokeswoman Claims Clinton Has Rare Brain Disease," *The Hill*, August 18, 2016.

23. Stephen Collinson, "Hillary Clinton Stumbles-Will Her Campaign Follow?" *CNN*, September 12, 2016.

24. Stephen Collinson and Jeremy Diamond, "Trump Finally Admits it: 'President Obama was Born in the United States," *CNN*, September 16, 2016.

25. Josh Voorhees, "All of Donald's Bitter Tweets," *Slate*, September 16, 2016.

26. Jacob Pramuk, "Trump: 'President Barack Obama was born in the United States. Period,'" *CNBC*, September 16, 2016.

27. Judy Ruiz, "This is the Worst Election, Ever," *CNN*, September 20, 2016.

28. Gregory Krieg, "Trump-Clinton Nasty? Not Compared to These Campaigns," *CNN*, September 23, 2016.

29. Kevin Swint, "Founding Father's Deity Campaign," *CNN*, August 22, 2008.
30. Jennifer Agiesta, "Post-Debate Poll: Hillary Clinton Takes Round One," *CNN*, September 27, 2016.
31. David A. Fahrenthold, "Trump Recorded Having Extremely Lewd Conversations About Women in 2005," *The Washington Post*, October 8, 2016.
32. Transcript: "Donald Trump's Taped Comments About Women," *New York Times*, October 8, 2016.
33. Alexander Burns, Maggie Haberman, and Jonathan Marten, "Donald Trump Apology Caps Day of Outrage over Leaked Tape," *New York Times*, October 7, 2016.
34. Susan Ferrechio, "Paul Ryan Cancels Saturday Appearance with Trump," *The Washington Examiner*, October 7, 2016.
35. Vaughn Hillyard, "Pence Cancels Event, Says He's 'Offended' by Trump's Comments," *NBC News*, October 8, 2016.
36. Eric Bradner, "Melania Trump: Donald Trump was 'egged on' into 'boy talk,'" *CNN*, October 18, 2016.
37. Shane Goldmacher, "Donald Trump Apologizes for Aggressive Crude Comments," *POLITICO*, October 8, 2016.
38. Ibid.
39. Ibid.
40. Eric Bradner, "Clinton's TPP Controversy," *CNN*, July 27, 2016.
41. Jake Sherman and John Bresnahan, "Ryan Abandons Trump," *POLITICO*, October 10, 2016.
42. Chas Danner, "Will Trump Go Nuclear in Debate-or Just Melt Down?" *New York Magazine*, October 9, 2016.
43. Ibid.
44. Chris Cillizza, "Winner and Losers from the Second Presidential Debate," *The Washington Post*, October 9, 2016.
45. Ibid.
46. Ibid.
47. Ibid.
48. BBC News, "Donald Trump's Mexico Wall," *BAC,* February 6, 2017.
49. Chico Harlan and Jerry Markon, "What it Will Take for President Trump to Deport Millions and Build the Wall," *The Washington Post*, November 9, 2016.

50. Noah Bierman, "Donald Trump's Muslim Ban was Removed for His Website, But It's Back," *The Los Angeles Times*, November 10, 2016
51. David Leonhardt, "The Real Voter Fraud," *New York Times*, November 8, 2016.
52. See Ari Berman, "Right to Vote? Wrong." *Sierra*, September/October, 2016, 34; and see also his book *Give Us the Ballot: The Modern Struggle for Voting Rights in America* (New York, Picador, 2016), and Zachary Roth, *The Great Suppression: Voting Rights, Corporate Cash, and the Conservative Assault on Democracy* (New York: Random House, 2016).
53. Susan Davis, "Mexican President Says He Told Trump Mexico Would Not Pay For A Wall," NPR, August 31, 2016, http://www.npr.org/2016/08/31/492132967/in-mexico-trump-reaffirms-u-s-right-to-protect-its-borders.
54. Yvonne Wingett Sanchez, "Donald Trump Back in Phoenix for 'Major Speech' on Inauguration," *The Arizona Republic*, August 29, 2016.
55. Joe Keohane, "The Cry-Baby," *POLITICO*, May/June 2016.
56. Ibid.
57. Ibid.
58. Ibid.
59. Dan Cassino, "This is How They Will Suggest the Election was Stolen," *Newsweek*, November 8, 2016.
60. Michael Barbaro, Maggie Haberman, and Alan Rappeport, "As American Sleeps, Donald Trump Seethes on Twitter," *New York Times*, September 30, 2016.
61. Becket Adams, "Ten of the Most Embarrassing Moments From Hillary Clinton's Campaign," *The Washington Examiner*, November 17, 2016.
62. Paul Musgrave, "Donald Trump is Normalizing Paranoia and Conspiracy Thinking," *The Washington Post*, January 12, 2017.
63. Ibid.
64. Ibid.
65. Ibid.
66. Ibid.
67. Ibid.
68. Trump said that the conspiracy against him includes Hillary meeting "in secret with international bankers to plot the destruction

of U.S. sovereignty," and enrich "global financial powers, her special-interest friends and her donors." See: Noah Bierman, "Harsh Words Threaten to Deepen Rift," *The Los Angeles Times*, October 16, 2016, A11.

69. Aaron Blake, "The Final Trump-Clinton Debate Transcript, Annotated," *The Washington Post*, October 19, 2016.

70. Ibid.

71. Editorial Board, "Trump is 'Unfit for the Presidency,'" *USA Today*, September 29, 2016.

72. Max Fisher, "Donald Trump's Threats to Reject Election Results Alarms Scholars," *The New York Times*, October 23, 2016.

73. Jonathan Swan, "Trump: 'I Don't Believe the Polls Anymore,'" *The Hill*, October 18, 2016.

74. Jose A. DelReal and Sean Sullivan, "Trump Claims Election is 'rigged,' and seems to Suggest Clinton was on Drugs at Debate, *The Washington Post*, October 15, 2016.

75. Eric Levitz, "Trump Says His Accusers are Pawns in a Globalist Conspiracy to End U.S. Sovereignty," *New York Magazine*, October 13, 2016.

76. Kevin Liptak, "Obama: Trump's Rigged Election Claim "Whining Before the Game is Over,'" *CNN*, October 18, 2016.

77. Mark Landler and Ashley Parker, "Stop 'Whining' and Trying to Discredit the Election, Obama Tells Trump," *New York Times*, October 19, 2016, A12.

78. Tim Starks, "Russian Hackers Trying to Influence U.S. Election," *POLITICO*, September 22, 2016.

79. Ashley Parker and David E. Sawyer, "Donald Trump Calls on Russia to Find Hillary Clinton's Missing Emails," *The New York Times*, July 27, 2016.

80. Alan Cole, "Details and Analysis of Donald Trump's Tax Plan," *Tax Foundation*, September 19, 2016.

81. Iwan Morgan, *The Age of Deficits: Presidents and Unbalanced Budgets From Jimmy Carter to George W. Bush* (Lawrence: University Press of Kansas, 2009).

82. Alex Altman and Jake T. Miller, "Why Donald Trump Picked Kellyanne Conway to Manage His Campaign," *TIME*, August 22, 2016.

83. Ryan Lizza, "Taming Trump." *The New Yorker*. October 17, 2016.

84. Ibid., p. 32.
85. Matt Flegenheimer and Ashley Parker, "A Night of Punchlines, Trump's Routine Prompts New York's Finest to Heckle," *The New York Times*, October 21, 2016, A18.
86. Ibid.
87. See Carol Felsenthal, "The Bride at Every Wedding." *The Huffington Post*, May 25, 2011.
88. Maxwell Tani, "Hillary Clinton 'on Defense' After Disastrous 72 Hours of Campaign," *Business Insider*, September 12, 2016, http://www.businessinsider.com/hillary-clinton-pneumonia-health-scare-scandal-2016-9.
89. Suffolk University, "Suffolk University/USA Today Poll Shows Clinton Leading Trump by 9 Points Nationwide," *Suffolk University*, October 26, 2016.
90. Brian Bennett, "Russia Spies an Opportunity," *The Los Angeles Times*, November 11, 2016, A4.
91. Melissa Healy, "Conspiracy Fears, Far From Fringe," *The Los Angeles Times*, November 5, 2016, 82.
92. "Conspiracy Fears", p. B2.
93. Louis Nelson, "Trump Tweets Praise of Putin," *POLITICO*, December 30, 2016.
94. Geraldine Cooper, Charlotte Krol, and Claire Lomas, "Donald Trump's Most Outrageous Quotes," *The Telegraph*, November 4, 2014
95. Ibid.
96. Ibid.
97. Ibid.
98. Editorial, "Mr. Trump's Impeachment Threat," *The New York Times*, November 4, 2016, A26.
99. Matt Apuzzo, Michael S. Schmidt, and Adam Goldman, "Emails Warrant No New Action Against Hillary Clinton, FBI Director Says," *The New York Times*, November 6, 2016.
100. Oliver Darcy, "Donald Trump Makes Closing Argument in Unconventional 2-Minute Ad," *Business Insider*, November 4, 2016.

CHAPTER 4

THE MEANING OF
THE 2016 ELECTION

The hardest thing about any political campaign is how to
win without proving that you are unworthy of winning.

—Adlai Stevenson[1]

November 9. Years of campaigning. Billions of dollars spent. A
squalid and depressing campaign. Two highly unpopular candidates.
And in the end, Donald J. Trump, a political outsider, a political
novice, a change candidate, ended up becoming the surprise, upset
winner.

He was the least experienced person ever elected to the presidency,
having no political or military background. He was also the oldest
person ever to be elected as president. His negatives were high yet
he won more electoral votes than George W. Bush won in 2000 or
2004. Who would have predicted it?

Figure 1. 2016 Presidential Election Map–270 electoral votes to win

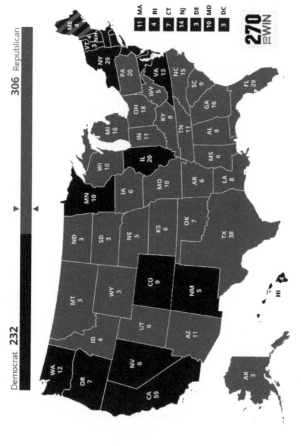

Source. http://www.270towin.com.

Table 3. Voter Turnout.

Year	% Turnout
1960	62.8%
1964	61.4%
1968	60.7%
1972	55.1%
1976	53.6%
1980	52.8%
1984	53.3%
1988	50.3%
1992	55.2%
1996	49.0%
2000	50.3%
2004	55.7%
2008	57.1%
2012	54.9%
2016	58%
Average Turnout	55.1%

TURNOUT

It was an ugly divisive race. Did it turn off voters? No. 2016 drew about the average percentage of voters, as past elections. Still, 58% for a presidential election is low when compared with most other democracies (see table 3).

WHY TRUMP SHOULD HAVE WON

One word: change. The time was right for a change. Eight years of one party should have given the opposition a leg up in a "throw the bums out" political season. More of the same was hard to sell, and so Trump, as the change candidate, had an advantage. In addition, over 70 percent of the public was unhappy with the direction in which the government/country was headed, so there too, advantage Trump. Trust in government was very low, and as the outsider who was not a professional politician, Trump did not suffer from beltway phobia.

Finally, the public—mostly left-wing supporters for Sanders and right-wing Tea Party supporters for Trump—were in the streets demanding something new. Starting with the base support of one of the major parties, and building on the discontent of the voters, Trump had all the ingredients for the electoral success.

WHY TRUMP ALMOST LOST

Three words: self-inflicted wounds. Has there ever been a major party nominee who shot himself in the foot more than Donald Trump? Space does not permit me to list the numerous ways in which Trump could have self-destructed. Trump said many things that could have led to his downfall, and despite running against a weak opponent with tons of heavy baggage, Trump seemed always to find a way to take attention away from Clinton's many weaknesses, and draw the spotlight onto himself as he said one outrageous thing after another. Trump nonetheless managed to pull victory out of the jaws of defeat.

WHY CLINTON SHOULD HAVE LOST

She was a poor campaigner; this had all the makings of a "change" election; Clinton was unpopular and not trusted; the Russians and the FBI gummed up the works for Clinton; and Clinton seemed perpetually under investigation by someone. She was vulnerable, and several of the more mainstream Republican hopefuls whom Trump defeated in the primaries, almost certainly would have beaten Clinton. She was poised to lose.

WHY CLINTON COULD HAVE WON

Five reasons: experience, money, organization, ground game, and Trump. Clinton's political experience was vast, and especially when compared to the political outsider, she simply knew more, had done more, and could draw on a vast network of associates to help her. The Clinton money machine was also a stable pipeline of funding that allowed her—early on—to build an experienced and capable campaign organization that built up a first-class ground game, giving her a decided advantage over the Trump campaign. And, of course, running against Trump seemed to be the gift that just kept giving. But it was not enough.

Amid Trump's surprising victory, let us not lose sight of the historic fact that despite her loss, a bit of history was made in the fact that a woman—for the first time—was the nominee for president of one of the major parties.

IT'S STILL THE ECONOMY, STUPID

Hillary Clinton was unable to maintain the "blue wall" of the rust belt states in America's manufacturing section of the Midwest. Workers, fearing the effects of globalization and economic change, abandoned the Democratic Party and voted for Trump in numbers sufficient to barely eke out Republican wins in Pennsylvania, Wisconsin, Michigan, and Ohio.[2] Economic uncertainty contributed mightily to the Trump victory.

IS DEMOGRAPHY DESTINY?

Democrats have long believed that demographic changes in the American population would guarantee electoral victories in the polls. The decline of white voters and the rise of voters of color seemed to favor the Democrats, giving them an insurmountable electoral edge against the Republicans. And while voters of color did overwhelmingly vote Democratic, a sufficient number of minority voters went with Trump adding to his sizeable margin of white voters who went with the Republican ticket. Demography is not destiny and in the future Democrats will have to work, and work hard, to maintain the loyalties of various minority voting groups.

HOW THE VOTE UNFOLDED

Many of the group voting patterns we expect played out in 2016, but there were several interesting wrinkles (see table 4).

The Gender Gap. Since 1980, there has been a persistent gender gap of about 8 points favoring the Democrats.[3] In 2016, that gap was 12 points.[4]

The Hispanic Gap. Donald Trump rose to political prominence by trashing Mexicans and immigrants. Did they make him pay a heavy price? Of the eight states with Hispanic populations larger than the national average, only Texas went to Trump.[5] Fewer than one in ten Republican voters were nonwhite.[6] The number of Hispanic eligible voters was roughly 25 million in 2016; by 2030 it will be 40 million.[7] Mitt Romney won Texas by 16 points in 2012,[8] and in 2016 Trump won the state by 9 points.[9]

Hispanics typically vote for the Democratic candidate at a 65% rate.[10] In 2016, that is the percent who went for Clinton.[11] Where was the surge of Hispanics who were angered by Trump's immigrant and Mexican bashing? In 2012, Obama got 71% of the Hispanic vote.[12] Why the drop-off in a year that should have been a huge Democratic vote?

African American Voters. African Americans have long been a stable part of the Democratic coalition, and in 2016 Hillary Clinton won 88% of African American votes—about average for a Democratic candidate.[13]

In exit polls from the election Trump did well with those wanting "change," but Clinton was seen as having the right experience (around 90%). Those "angry" with the federal government went overwhelmingly (over 75%) for Trump.[14] And the key reason voters gave in defense of their vote was "dislike" of the other candidate," confirming that both candidates had very high unfavorable ratings.

The White Male Vote. Donald Trump did very well with white male voters. Although as a voting group, white males are in decline, they rallied behind Trump and served as the core group of his base. He got 58% of the male vote to Clinton's 41%.[15] As CNN commentator Van Jones noted, this election was a "white-lash."[16]

Millennials. Millennials helped elect Barack Obama—twice. They voted for Clinton 54% to Trump's 37%,[17] but turnout was not what Clinton expected. The 18–29 year old age group comprised only 19% of the voters in 2016.[18]

Table 4a. 2016 Voting Blocks.

		TRUMP	CLINTON	Gap	% of Vote
Sex	Men	53	41	12T	48%
	Women	42	54	12C	52%
Race	White	58	37	21T	70%
	Black	8	88	80C	12%
	Hispanic	29	65	36C	11%
	Asian	29	65	36C	4%
Age	18-29	37	54	17C	19%
	30-44	42	50	8C	25%
	45-64	53	44	9T	40%
	65 + over	52	45	7T	16
Education	HS or less	51	45	6T	18%
	Some College/ Associate Degree	52	43	9T	32
	College Grad	45	49	4C	32%
	Post Grad Study	37	58	21C	18%

Table 4b. 2016 Voting Blocks (*Cont'd*).

		TRUMP	CLINTON	Gap	% of Vote
Income	Under $30,000	41	53	12C	17%
	$30-49,999	42	51	9C	19%
	$50-99,999	50	46	4T	31%
	$100-199,999	48	48	0	24%
	$200,000-249,999	48	48	0	4%
	$250,000 or over	48	46	2T	6%
Urban/Rural	Over 50,000	35	59	24C	34%
	Suburbs	50	45	5T	49%
	Small City/Rural	62	34	28T	17
Married	Yes	53	43	10T	59%
	No	38	55	17C	41%
What was the most important issue in the campaign?	FP	34	60	26C	13%
	Immigration	64	33	31T	13%
	Economy	42	52	10C	52%
	Terrorism	57	39	18T	18%

According to exit polls (adapted from *New York Times*, November 9, 2016).

College-Educated Voters. Traditionally a part of the Republican coalition in 2016, college graduates preferred Clinton by 4% and people with postgraduate educations went 58-37% for Clinton.[19]

The Rust Belt. From the beginning, Donald Trump believed he could win over traditionally Democratic states in the rust belt. He was right. Pennsylvania, Ohio, Wisconsin all went for Trump. This was a significant reason why Trump won.

Republican voters came home; Democratic voters stayed home. White working-class voters went for Trump and, astonishingly, 29% of Hispanics voted Trump.[20] The Obama coalition did not coalesce for Clinton (it truly was an Obama, not a Democratic Party. coalition). Non-college-educated women went for Trump.[21] White voters went 58% for Trump, 53% of men voted for Trump, 67% of those without a college degree went Trump.[22] Young, black, and Hispanic voters let Clinton down with lower turnout than expected.[23] Change voters— of whom there were many, went for Trump. Angry voters—again, many—voted for Trump. A number of people voted against Clinton. The rust belt went for Trump. Plus enthusiasm won out over organization in voter turnout as Trump's voters were more passionate and committed to their candidate than Clinton's supporters.

POLITICAL REALIGNMENT?

Do the results of the election portend significant shifts in voting trends, even a political realignment? White working-class voters, a staple of the Democratic coalition, voted for Trump, while college-educated voters who are traditionally Republican went for Clinton.

Political realignments, deep fundamental shifts in parties on loyalties and ideological change, occur rarely. The last true realignment occurred in 1932–1934 when Franklin D. Roosevelt and the Democrats swept into office during the Great Depression, and the

Democrats became America's dominant party for roughly forty years. That realignment began to break down in the 1970s when Southern states shifted from the Democratic to the Republican Party. Since then, the partisan back-and-forth has not brought on a new realignment. The country may be ripe for a new party system.

So much of Trump's populist support came from less-educated, white working-class males who felt they were the victims of globalization. Their manufacturing jobs—a guarantee of a middle-class existence—have evaporated, been outsourced, and disappeared. These are voters who feel economic and job insecurity, have been hit hard by stagnant wages, are sometimes mocked (for living in "flyover states"), who resent the elites who have benefited from the recovery while they have floundered.

Clinton had a difficult time attracting these traditionally Democratic voters. These "downwardly mobile white workers" flocked to Trump. Of these voters, Robert Packer writes:

> "Working class," meanwhile, has become a euphemism. It once suggested productivity and sturdiness. Now it means downwardly mobile, poor, even pathological. A significant part of the W.W.C. has succumbed to the ills that used to be associated with the black urban "underclass": intergenerational poverty, welfare, debt, bankruptcy, out-of-wedlock births, trash entertainment, addiction, jail, social distrust, political cynicism, bad health, unhappiness, early death. The heartland towns that abandoned the Democrats in the eighties to bask in Ronald Reagan's morning sunlight; the communities that Sarah Palin, on a 2008 campaign stop in Greensboro, North Carolina, called "the best of America. . . the real America"—those places were hollowing out, and politicians didn't seem to notice. A great inversion occurred. The dangerous, depraved cities gradually became safe for clean-living professional families who happily paid thousands of dollars to prep their kids for the gifted-and-talented

test, while the region surrounding Greensboro lost tobacco, textiles, and furniture-making, in a rapid collapse around the turn of the millennium, so that OxyContin and disability and home invasions had taken root by the time Palin saluted those towns, in remarks that were a generation out of date.[24]

These voters are the most pessimistic people in the country, and they are changing our political arithmetic.[25] Republican political strategists Steve Schmidt argues that the divide in America used to be left versus right, now it is up versus down.[26] While liberal versus conservative still matters, the real cleavage is between those who can benefit from globalization's changes and those left behind. This will only get more pressing in the coming years as automation, robotics, and driverless cars put more of the working class out of work and on unemployment. This trend suggests the rise of "Rust Belt Republican" in states like Ohio, Michigan, and even Pennsylvania.

The loyalties which different groups show to a political party can be deep and long running. But coalitions aren't permanent, and at times, over various issues, a voting bloc—never totally monolithic— could migrate to the opposition party. Such, for example, is the case of the once solidly Democratic South shifting—beginning in the mid-1960s due to Lyndon B. Johnson and the Democratic Party's embrace of civil rights reform—to the Republicans, creating the solid Republican South.[27]

One reversal does not a permanent reversal of loyalties make, but a shift of note did take place in the 2016 election that—if it endures —could spell a realignment of our party system. In this election, many working-class, blue-collar voters voted for Trump. This group usually voted for Democrats. On the other side of the equation, college-educated voters—a traditional part of the Republican base —went for Clinton. Is this a temporary or long-term shift?

Political Scientists Pick the Winners

Many political scientists believe that campaigns matter little, candidates are only of marginal importance, and campaign strategies do little to change votes. These folks believe that larger forces —the state of the economy, the mood of the public, or levels of presidential popularity—shape election outcomes more than the candidates. Are they right?

At each presidential election, the community of vote predictors issue their predictions, and some of the more prominent ones are featured in a pre-election volume of *PS*, published by the American Political Science Association (APSA). 2016 was no exception. What did their different models predict?

The "polarized party" model looks at the deep divisions in the two parties. These models predict—not very helpfully—a close race. The "sluggish economic growth" models "suggest a Trump victory." The "public mood" models also favor Trump and the Republicans. The "presidential approval" models predict a close race. And the "pre-convention preference poll" models favor Clinton and the Democrats.[28]

A summary of the forecasts do favor a Clinton victory as well as Democratic gains in the House (from between no change and a 32-seat pickup) and the Senate (from 4-7 seat pickup). Oh boy, were we wrong! Trump won the election and the Democrats picked up only a handful of seats in the House and could not win control of the Senate.

One political historian did correctly predict Trump's win—Allan Lichtman, whose prediction "isn't based on horse-race polls, shifting demographics or his own political opinions. Rather, he uses a system of true/false statements he calls the 'Keys to the White House' to determine his predicted winner."[29]

Most of the "experts" predicted a close race, but most overestimated the percent of Clinton votes (most had her just above the 50% mark). No matter which key variable was selected on which scholars based their conclusions—state of the economy, time for a change vote, unemployment rate, direction the country is going, state-by-state analysis, popularity of the sitting president, poll watchers—virtually all gave Clinton a slight edge.

EXPLAINING TRUMP'S RISE

How are we to explain and understand the rise of Trump? For years, starting with the Reagan presidency, blossoming during the Bill Clinton presidency, becoming fully toxic under Speaker Newt Gingrich, condoning the hatred sometimes evident in the Tea Party movement, and going to excess in the Obama years, the Republicans created a climate and a culture in which they began consciously channeling paranoia,[30] racial animus,[31] birther conspiracies,[32] a culture of partisan hatred.[33]

The Republican Party set the table, and created the conditions that made the rise of Trump possible. As Fareed Zakaria wrote:

> There have always been radicals on both sides of the political spectrum. But what is different about the conservative movement is that, since the 1990s, some of its most distinguished mainstream members have embraced the rhetoric and tactics of the extremes. A memo put out by Newt Gingrich's political action committee that decade urged candidates to use savage rhetoric against their Democratic opponents. Some of the recommended words were "failure," "pathetic," "disgrace" and "incompetent." In the past ... Trump has called Mitt Romney a "failed candidate," Jeb Bush "pathetic," Sen. Lindsey Graham (R-S.C.) "a disgrace" and Obama "totally incompetent." [34]

And Zakaria concludes his argument writing:

Here is a much simpler explanation for Donald Trump: Republicans have fed the country ideas about decline, betrayal and treason. They have encouraged the forces of ant-intellectualism, obstructionism, and populism. They have flirted with bigotry and racism. Trump merely chose to unashamedly embrace all of it, saying plainly what they were hinting at for years. In doing so, he hit a jackpot.[2]7

The Republican Party created Trump. He exploited the climate set by Republicans, but he did not create this climate. It had been building for years. Some people had real concerns and complaints; others had found in Trump a champion of their prejudices.

A populist tsunami had been building on the right for twenty years. Many Americans hurt by the recession, locked in low wage, stagnant paying jobs, and hurt by the larger forces of globalization turned against the establishment. Their genuine concerns became part of the Trump movement. But so did racist, nativist, sexist elements. In Atlantic.com, conservative David Frum wrote:

> Trump has appealed to white identity more explicitly than any national political figure since George Wallace. But whereas Wallace was marginalized first within the Democratic Party, and then within national politics, Trump has increasingly been accommodated. Yes, Trump was often fiercely denounced by rivals and insiders in the earlier part of the campaign. But since effectively securing the nomination, that criticism had quieted. Trump is running not to be president of all Americans, but to be the clan leader of white Americans. Those white Americans who respond to his message head his abusive comments, not as evidence of his unfitness for office, but as proof of his commitment to their tribe. [35]

In 2016, the Republican mainstream ended up coming home to

Trump after initially being suspicious of their party's nominee. Roughly 90% of Republicans ended up voting for Trump.[36]

TRUMP'S IMPACT ON THE REPUBLICAN PARTY

So what awaits the Republican Party in an era of Trump? A civil war? Reconciliation? Divorce of the Trumpkins from the Establishment? A return to (ab)normalcy? Capture by the radical fringe?

Trump exposed deep fissures between the Republican establishment and the grassroot populists who flocked to Trump. Those cleavages will not disappear, but do they spell doom for the party?

It would be hard to fully purge the Trumpkins from the party. Trump's supporters have already been placed in key positions in the Republican National Committee, they comprise a key voting bloc within the party, they are egged on and their views are legitimized by Fox News and talk radio voices on the right, they staff key positions in the Trump administration—there is no indication that in a postelection period they will be going away.

What impact would Trump have on the long-term interests of the Republican Party? Was he a "stain" that could be washed away, or a "tattoo" that left a permanent mark?

Populism is sometimes popular—until it gets elected. Then the illiberal tendencies often clash with the American tradition of liberal democracy. The search for a strongman savior to solve our problems may seem attractive in difficult times, but rarely has the strongman been the solution to our problems and usually ends up being a problem to be solved.

Has Donald Trump energized or damaged the Republican Party? Part of the answer to that question depends on whether Trumpism takes hold in the Party. Trump, the individual, may be an aberration, a one-off, impossible to replicate and therefore a one-time-only candidate.

Should the GOP return to its pre-Trump positions of small government, free trade, low taxes, and entitlement cuts, or should it grow the base by opening the party to nonwhite groups, welcoming them into the fold? Or can a Trump presidency secure a new governing coalition for the Republicans?

Trump has exploited the rift in society of the ins versus the outs, the haves versus the have nots, the educated verses less educated, urban versus rural, the beneficiaries versus the downtrodden. Trump's followers are not monolithic. One part of his coalition is made up of those who were battered and bruised by the recession of 2007–2008. They were deeply hurt by the recession, globalization, the loss of manufacturing jobs, stymied by income stagnation, and left with little hope. These angry voters have a legitimate beef with the establishment. Their incomes decline as income inequality grows, their future seems dim while a small minority become super rich. Those are people who need to be listened to; whose very real problems need to be addressed.

But there is the other part of the Trump coalition: racists, xenophobes, misogynists, nativists, those Hillary Clinton indelicately referred to as "deplorables."[37] Their anger and resentment over an African American (or a woman) in the White House, immigrants, and other such prejudice drove the Trump bus, and they are still out there, angry and contemptuous of society.

In 1984, Ronald Reagan won 56% of the white vote, won 44 states, and won the election in a landslide.[38] In 2012, Mitt Romney won 59% of the white vote and lost the election.[39] Moving ahead, the Republican Party simply has to broaden its appeal to minorities or it may decline electorally. But how will that change the party?

To some it was the party of Lincoln; to still others, it was the party of Reagan. Today, the Republican Party is the party of Trump.

THE DEMOCRATS AFTER TRUMP'S WIN

Many Democrats will argue that 2016 is the "last white election," that by 2020 (and beyond), the electorate belongs to them.[40] But playing this waiting game (waiting for the demographics to catch up with the politics) has its dangers. It frees the Democrats to dismiss self-analysis, as they simply wait for the next election.

But if they are smart, they will try to figure out how they can offer policies that attempt to reclaim the white working-class voters who were once theirs. Simply writing off the working class is tantamount to following in Republican footsteps as they write off people of color—it simply makes no sense.

The Democratic Party needs to do some serious soul-searching lest it become merely the "boutique issue party," appealing to this group and that group, but never actually standing up for ideas.

After the 1964 rout of Republican Barry Goldwater, forecasts of the death of the Republican Party were common. Four years later, they won the White House.[41] The same fears were manifested by the Democrats after 1972 nominee George McGovern got routed by Richard Nixon. Four years later, they too won the White House.[42] So reports of the death of the 2016 Democratic Party may well be premature.

DID RUSSIA HELP ELECT DONALD TRUMP?

Seventeen U.S. intelligence agencies plus the intelligence units from several NATO countries confirmed that Russia had been actively meddling in elections in Germany, Great Britain, and the United

States.[43] The goal? To breakup NATO and undermine democracy.[44] England's "Brexit" vote and the NATO bashing of candidate Donald Trump were the beneficiaries of Mr. Putin's mischief.[45] Putin loathed Clinton.[46] And the bizarre bromance between Putin and Trump was for the wily Russian, merely a marriage of convenience—it suited his ends.[47] Putin viewed Trump as a "useful fool."[48] In his national security briefings Trump was informed of the Russian interference in the election, which seemed only to bolster Trump's impression of Putin.[49]

The Russian *DUMA* (legislature) was in session when Trump's election was announced. The hall burst out in a round of applause.[50] Why did Russia prefer Trump to Clinton? Did Russia end up the big winner in 2016?

DID THE FBI HELP ELECT DONALD TRUMP?

The FBI's unprecedented intrusion into the 2016 election kept the issue of Hillary Clinton's e-mail problem in front of the American voter, and in spite of their refusal to charge Clinton with any crime, it reinforced Trump's "crooked Hillary" narrative.[51]

THE BLUE WALL COMES TUMBLING DOWN

Many commentators argue that it was the collapse of the Democratic Party's "blue wall" that led to the defeat of Hillary Clinton.[52] The Clinton campaign believed that it had an insurance policy against a Trump surge: the states of Wisconsin, Michigan, and Pennsylvania, the blue wall that would block a Trump advance.[53]

But as the Industrial Belt morphed into the Rust Belt, and as union membership dropped (in 1964, 37% of Ohio worker were union members, by 2016 that number had dropped to 12%;[54] and much the same was true of Michigan, Pennsylvania, and Wisconsin),[55] the solidly Democratic blue wall began to crack. In 2016, it fell.

In Wisconsin, Democrats had won seven consecutive presidential contests; the same was true in Michigan; and in Pennsylvania Democratic presidents won six straight contests.[56] In Wisconsin, Clinton lost by just 27,257 votes (47.9% to 46.9%).[57] In Michigan, Clinton lost by only 11, 612 (47.6% to 47.3%).[58] And in Pennsylvania Clinton lost by 68,236 votes (48.8% to 47.6%).[59]

DID GENDER DOOM CLINTON?

Did gender hurt Clinton? While few voters would publicly admit that the fact that Hillary Clinton was a woman might prevent them from voting for her, several studies suggest that a woman might not be as electorally acceptable to as many voters as we think. [60] It is hard to quantify this bias, but it might have had a marginal impact in Clinton's vote. And even 1% would have dramatically impacted the results of the election.

DID VOTER SUPPRESSION MATTER?

Did voter suppression efforts work? A Republican "block the vote" effort to suppress votes was a part of their victory strategy.[61] It was called "Operation Ratf***ked" by Republican strategist Ben Ginsberg,[62] and was aimed at minorities and young voters whose participation in the election they hoped to limit.

The key to this strategy was the 2013 Supreme Court decision *Shelby County v. Holder* where the Court dramatically weakened Section 5 of the Voting Rights Act (which required federal preapproval of changes in voting laws in areas with a history of discrimination). In gutting that portion of the Act, the Court opened a door to voter suppression that a number of Republican-controlled states used to limit voting access. How? Higher hurdles to voting, new ID rules, shortening the hours polls were open, reducing or eliminating same-day registration, all done in the name of reducing voter fraud that did not exist in any significant way. Most of the more restrictive states were in the East and South, while the Western states were more open or relaxed in their voting requirements. And Republican-controlled states clearly dominated in their willingness to embrace voting restrictions.[63] It was expected that these new laws could depress Latino vote, as well as the African American and the millennial vote.[64]

Several of the new voting restrictions were thrown out by state courts, but many remained.[65] Thirty-two states have some form of voter ID laws, and most of them went for Trump. Accident? You be the judge.

From 2000 to 2016, we have seen a steady rise in the number of states "requesting" ID (from under 14 in 2000 to over 30 in 2016) and the number "requiring" ID (0 in 2000 to 9 in 2016).

This effort by Republicans to limit voting was deliberate and coordinated.[66] If you have any doubts, here is the Facebook response to this effort by Todd Allbaugh, a Wisconsin staff aide to a Republican state legislature:

> You wanna know why I left the Republican Party as it exists today? Here it is; this was the last straw: I was in the closed Senate Republican Caucus when the final round of multiple Voter ID bills were being discussed. A handful of the GOP Senators were giddy about the ramifications and literally singled out the prospects of suppressing minority and college voters. Think about that for a minute. Elected officials planning and happy to help deny a fellow American's constitu-

tional right to vote in order to increase their own chances to hang onto power.[67]

And in 2013, Don Yelton, a North Carolina Republican Party county precinct chairman said that his state's voter ID laws would "kick the Democrats in the butt."[68] Florida's Republican Party Chairman Jim Green admitted that his state's Voter ID law was designed to suppress Democratic votes, saying "we've got to cut down on early voting because early voting is not good for us."[69]

DID BIG MONEY MATTER IN 2016?

Citizens United and other Court decisions striking down limitations on money in the political process did open the floodgates of money into politics, but 2016 was the year when money seems *not* to have been a major factor. Donald Trump semi-self-funded his race, ran an effective Twitter-outreach campaign, and relied on an estimated billion dollars of free publicity from the media.

2016 was also the year that Bernie Sanders demonstrated that one could run a credible presidential campaign relying on a large number of small donors. Hillary Clinton ran a conventional big-money campaign, and she proved the exception in this exceptional election year. Hilary Clinton outspent Trump by a wide margin, as did outside spending groups. Clinton's team raised roughly $500,000,000 and outside groups raised an additional $200,000,000 for Clinton.[70] Trump raised (not counting the value of the free media he received) about $250,000,000 and outside spending on behalf of Trump was around $75,000,000.[71] Clearly, money did not determine the outcome of the 2016 race.

DID MEDIA—NEW AND OLD—IMPACT THE ELECTION?

Trust in the media, especially the mainstream media, was low. Many voters, especially younger voters, got their news from social media. There was thus a new vulnerability to "fake news" which proliferated the blogosphere. Given the fact that voters felt they could not rely on standard media outlets, a door was opened for candidates—and Donald Trump masterfully used this to his advantage—to create the news and the narrative.[72]

There were wide variations by party membership in trust of the mainstream media. And while trust declined by both Democrats and Republicans (in 1997, about 64% of Democrats had some trust in the media, by 2016 that number dropped to 51%; for Republicans in that period, trust fell from 41% to around 14%), Republicans clearly had more negative impressions of the media.[73]

Recent campaigns have clearly been more "social media" oriented. Almost half of American say they get their news from social media "often" or "sometimes," and that number has risen with each of the past five presidential elections.[74]

PARTY POOPER

The Republicans went into the November 8 election with majorities in both the House (247 to 188) and Senate (54-44 with two Independents, Bernie Sanders and Angus King caucusing with the Democrats). As election day approached, Republicans wondered how much Donald Trump might hurt their candidates in down-ticket races. As it turns out, while the Republicans did lose seats in the House and Senate, the numbers were well within what one might normally expect.

Voting in 2016 reinforced the hyperpartisan model of voting which suggests that the parties are becoming more divided and more partisan. This creates a gulf between the two parties in which each party increasingly sees the opposition in more harsh and negative ways. Cooperation, bargaining, and compromise—so vital for a healthy, functioning democracy—becomes near impossible in such conditions.

It is common for Americans to complain about the quality of our presidential candidates, but 2016 surpassed all records. More people voted against a candidate than for one. In 2004 a majority of Democrats said their primary motivation was to vote against George W. Bush, but never before have both candidates received a higher combined "voted against" score than in 2016.[75]

THE NON-PARTY PARTIES

In 2016 outsiders, nonparty members, sought to seize the party nomination in the Democratic (Bernie Sanders) and Republican (Donald Trump) parties. It is possible to do this because all one has to do to seek the nomination is register in that party (which Sanders did on the morning he filed for his candidacy) and run. If you get enough votes in the party caucuses and primaries, you get the nomination, and the party hierarchy can do little to stop you.

Bernie Sanders was an Independent Socialist until he sought the Democratic nomination. Donald Trump has changed political parties at least five times.[76] But they each strategically calculated that regardless of the party insiders, a wide-open nomination battle might be winnable. And so, leading the ticket on a major party is a prize that virtually anyone can seek. And the establishment favorite (Jeb in 2016) can be left out in the cold.

Is this a good or bad thing? It may be good because an open, dynamic nomination gives the members of the party—the rank-and-file—the opportunity to select *their* nominee, absent too much interference from the higher-ups. Thus, an outsider can capture the hearts and minds of members and truly be the representative of the members of that party.

But others see it as a bad thing because it may be the party bosses and regulars who have the long-term interests of the party in mind, who can select the candidate that best represents the party itself, or who has a legitimate chance of winning the election. Party insiders *would not* have selected Sanders or Trump, yet both had fairly large, committed followings. But in both cases, their followers were deeply committed, but not necessarily representations of the larger party across the nation.

So which is better, a wide open race or one that is filtered through the party leadership? If "the people" had spoken, it might have been Bernie Sanders versus Donald Trump. If the party insiders had spoken it would been Jeb Bush versus Hillary Clinton.

What kind of party system has virtually no control over who shall be the party's nominee for president? Is it even "really" a party if *anyone* can come in and, with enough votes, capture the prize?

Rural Versus Urban

In 2016, Hillary Clinton won only 472 counties while Donald Trump won nearly 3,000.[77] That sure sounds like a landslide, but on closer inspection Clinton won dense, urban areas, while Trump won more sparsely populated rural areas. Clinton's 472 counties accounted for roughly two-thirds of the nation's total economic output.[78] Are there then two Americas?

Trump's List of Enemies

Questions of Trump's character and temperament were raised again on election night when supporter (and former "The Apprentice" competitor) Omarosa Manigault went public with Donald Trump's "enemies list." Not since the days of the disgraced Richard Nixon has a president had - and used - an enemies list. "It's so great," she said, "our enemies are making themselves clear so that when we get into the White House, we know where we stand." Then, referring to a tweet by Republican Senator Lindsey Graham in which he announced he had voted for Evan McMullin, that "If [Graham] felt his interests was with that candidate, God Bless him. I would never judge anybody for exercising their right to and the freedom to choose who they want. But let me just tell you, Mr. Trump has a long memory and we're keeping a list."[79]

PANTS ON FIRE IN A POST-TRUTH WORLD

Can we trust politicians? Hillary Clinton is in effect a career politician. Donald Trump, in contrast, is anything but a politician. So who is more truthful? Who has more of what Stephen Colbert calls "truthiness?"[80]

PolitiFact has done the heavy lifting for us on the truth meter (see tables 5 and 6), and it seems like there are many discrepancies between what is said and the facts.

Table 5. Donald Trump's Questionable Relationship to the Truth

Donald Trump PolitiFact scorecard	
True	14 (4%)
Mostly True	37 (11%)
Half True	49 (15%)
Mostly False	63 (19%)
False	111 (34%)
Pants on Fire	57 (17%)

Source. *PolitiFact,* http://www.politifact.com/truth-o-meter/lists/people/
comparing-hillary-clinton-donald-trump-truth-o-met/]

WHO IS THE REAL TRUMP?

Trump ran by dividing (and attacking parts of) the nation; his election night speech however was gracious and inclusive. Will a Trump presidency further divide us or unite us?

George W. Bush ran for president in 2000 as "a uniter, not a divider." He ended up being a very divisive president.[81] In 2008, Barack Obama said, "There is no red America, there is no blue America, there is only the United States of America." He too turned out to be a divisive president.[82] What of Trump?

Table 6. How Does Clinton Compare with Trump Regarding Truth?

Hillary Clinton PolitiFact scorecard	
True	72 (25%)
Mostly True	76 (26%)
Half True	69 (24%)
Mostly False	40 (14%)
False	29 (10%)
Pants on Fire	7 (2%)

Source. PolitiFact, http://www.politifact.com/truth-o-meter/lists/people/comparing-hillary-clinton-donald-trump-truth-o-met/]

ANOTHER OUTSIDER

America loves outsiders. We think they are not infected with the "beltway disease" and that they will ride into town like the sheriff in an old Western movie, clean up the mess ("drain the swamp"), and fix all out problems. It is a romantic vision of a world where good triumphs over evil, and one man (yes, man) can save us. Problem is, that just isn't reality.

We've tried time and again, to bring in outsiders, but they are part of the problem, not the solution. Inexperienced outsiders have not done well in the White House. Yet the romantic attraction remains.

Since 1976, we've elected six outsiders and one insider (George H.W. Bush). You decide if the outsiders were our salvation or not (see table 7). In *The Republic*, Plato argued that leading the *polis*

Table 7. Presidential Insiders and Outsiders

Year	President	Insider	Outsider
1976	Carter		✓✓
1980	Reagan		✓✓
1984	Reagan	(✓)	✓✓
1988	HW Bush	✓	
1992	Clinton		✓✓
1996	Clinton	(✓)	✓✓
2000	W Bush		✓
2004	W Bush	(✓)	✓✓
2008	Obama		✓
2012	Obama	(✓)	✓
2016	Trump		✓

required years of focused training.[83] Americans believe that insiders are part of the problem.

If we remove those incumbents running for reelection (four) there is only one insider, George H.W. Bush, who has won the presidency in the past forty years.

THE CHARACTER QUESTION

This was an election decided more on personality and character than policies and ideas. As such, the voters were presented with the choice of two "character challenged" candidates. Hillary Clinton generated very low scores on the trust meter, and Trump's comments on women, Mexicans, immigrants, war heroes, the handicapped, and so forth left many voters disgusted.

In judging a presidential candidate, there are three elements of "character" to consider: public, private, and constitutional character. Public character is one's moral and ethical compass in pursuit of the public good. It is about trying to do the right thing. Private character involves what one does, how one behaves in his or her private (i.e., family) life. Constitutional character involves "the disposition to act, and motivate others to act, according to principles that constitute the democratic process..." and "includes such questions as sensitivity to basic rights, respect for due process... willingness to agree to accept responsibility, tolerance of opposition, and most importantly a commitment to candor."[84]

How do the two candidates rate on these measures of character? Sadly, on all three categories of character Clinton and Trump are found wanting. Hillary Clinton's public character has been repeatedly called into question on matters from her e-mails to Benghazi. In private character, the uses (and abuses?) of the Clinton Foundation also raised serious questions. On constitutional questions, Clinton fares considerably better, ranking high on most measures.

Donald Trump has a long history of shady business dealings,[85] and could be seen as ranking low in public character. His record on private character is abysmal as the thrice-married Trump objectifies and insults women regularly,[86] and brags about his indiscretions.[87] Perhaps most frightening are Trump's low marks on constitutional character, as his unwillingness to accept the results of the election,[88] his constant trashing of political opponents,[89] and his belittling of due process ("we're gonna have a deportation force")[90] indicate.

Trump's open contempt for the norms of our constitutional republic—evident in his threat to imprison his opponent;[91] stated goals of narrowing press freedoms by changing liberal laws; call for the resumption of torture; goal to ban all Muslim immigrants;[92] questioning the independence of the judiciary and the fairness of an Indiana-born federal judge who Trump claimed to be biased because of the judge's Mexican parentage;[93] his plan to round up and deport millions of undocumented immigrants;[94] as well as his refusal to say that he would accept the outcome of the election[95]— all speak to Trump's failure to fulfill even the most minimum of constitutional ethics.

With two candidates who were seriously "character challenged," they seemed to cancel each other out on this issue.

PRESIDENT TRUMP'S "LEVEL OF POLITICAL OPPORTUNITY"

A president's *level of political opportunity,*[96] sometimes referred to as *political capital,* is the context in which a president governs and the political fuel he has to ignite the engine of governing. In calculating a president's political opportunity, we should consider:

1) **The President's Party in Congress:** Is the party of the President the majority party in Congress? If so, by how much? A large majority opens a door to power, a slim majority gives the

president some limited leverage, and when the opposition controls Congress, the president has very limited political clout.

2) The Results of the Last Election: Did the president win in a landslide? Was it a squeaker? The bigger the electoral victory, the more the president can claim a *mandate to govern.*

3) What Type of Election was it? Elections based on policy matter more to a president's success than do elections based on a personality, (see Reagan's 1980 victory which gave him high opportunity versus 1984 when he had little).

4) Did the President have Coattails? Did the president run ahead of members of Congress in their districts? If so, the president may argue that he or she helped Congressperson X electorally; If not, (e.g., Clinton in 1992) members feel less dependent on and indebted to the president.

5) Nature of the Opposition: Is the opposition cohesive and unified against the president (e.g., Republicans during the Obama years), or are they willing to work *with* the president?

6) The Public's Mood: Does the public demand action? Is public trust in government high?

7) The President's Skill and Experience: While not enough, skill and experience do matter.

8) The President's "Power Sense": Does the president know how to pull on the levels of power? When to? When not to? Does the president have a good "strategic sense?"

Measuring Trump's Opportunity

1) **The President's Party in Congress:** Donald Trump comes to office with majorities in both the House and the Senate.

Having unified government should help him achieve some of his legislative goals.

2) **Results of the Last Election:** It was a hard fought election, and Trump won by a significant margin. While no landslide, Trump did convincingly beat Hillary Clinton. But while Trump won in the Electoral College, Clinton won the popular vote, thus neutralizing some of the glow on Trump's victory. Two days before the election, Donald Trump tweeted, "The Electoral College is a disaster for a democracy."[97] With Clinton beating Trump for the popular vote, that is probably something Trump and Clinton might agree on.

3) **Type of Election:** The 2016 race was dominated by the oversized personality of Donald Trump. Issues, while of some importance, paled in comparison to the personal. Hillary was unpopular and untrustworthy, Donald was unpopular and belligerent. It was a contest of character (or lack thereof), not issues. This added nothing to the victory.

4) **Coattails:** Republicans lost seats in the House and Senate in 2016, but not many. Trump seemed to have coattails, but fairly short ones. Trump ran behind most Republican legislators in their states or districts, thus his coattails, such as they were, will not help him govern. However, those Republican Senate candidates who stood squarely with Trump (Ron Johnson in Wisconsin, Richard Burr in North Carolina, and Roy Blunt in Missouri)[98] did better than those who distanced themselves from Trump (Mark Kirk of Illinois and Kelly Ayotte in New Hampshire).[99]

5) **The Opposition:** The Democrats will be a thorn in Trump's side, but it remains to be seen just how obstructionist they will try to be, and how unified they are in the opposition to Trump. They will not—thankfully—be the mirror image of the Republicans, but they will not give Trump a free pass either.

6) **The Public's Mood:** Trump won the votes of angry voters. Can he keep them at bay, or will they eventually turn on him?

Trust in government is low, and how long will it be before Trump takes full ownership of the government, and will he then be seen as part of the problem? What if he can't get his promises enacted, or the wall built, or ... Trust in Government was at an all-time low; Trust in Trump was low; public cynicism was high; and political partisanship was high. The public was in an angry mood, unhappy with the direction in which the nation was moving, yet unwilling to lend support to the new president to achieve policy goals.

7) **Skills and Experience:** Donald Trump has never held political office, and while experience in politics is not a requirement for the job, it is certainly of use. Only four of his predecessors never held elective office (Zachary Taylor, Ulysses Grant, and Dwight Eisenhower who were generals, and Herbert Hoover who served as a Cabinet official). The world of politics is vastly different from the world of business—can Trump successfully make that transition?

8) **Trump's "Power Sense":** With his skill at self-promotion, Trump knows how to attract attention. He seems to have a good power sense, and that was part of the reason he did so well in the primaries and general election. But government is more than just posing and attacking. Does Trump have a good political or governing power sense?

Trust in government has been steadily dropping since the 1970s. While there was a bump up in trust following 9/11, it did not last long. In the early 1960s, roughly three in four Americans said they had a fairly high level of trust in government. By 2016, that number hovered in the 20% mark.[100] How can anyone govern when trust in government is so low?

DONALD TRUMP'S OPPORTUNITY SCORECARD

Table 8. Trump's Level of Political Opportunity.

Positive	Neutral	Negative
#s 1	#s 2, 3, 4, 7, 8	#s 5, 6
1	5	2

Table 8 suggests that Donald Trump's level of political opportunity and his political capital will not be exceptionally high. Circumstances could change, as they did for George W. Bush due to the 9/11 attack, but in general, Trump's opportunity level should be marginal.

Can Trump govern? Fanning flames of fear, anger, and negativity might have been a winning campaign strategy, but can that be converted into a governing strategy? What are the consequences of a largely negative campaign on the prospect for governing?

From day one, President Trump will face a country in which roughly half the people are against him. His political capital will be limited.

THE BIG AMERICAN ZIG-ZAG

A divided nation, a nation that lurches from left to right, the United States does not have a clear sense of where it wants to go. The nation has lurched from right (Ronald Reagan, George H.W. Bush) to left (Bill Clinton), back to the right (George W. Bush), then left (Barack Obama)[101], and now, back to the right with Trump.

Some may see this as a healthy sign, others as a symptom of

America's political schizophrenia. We just don't know who we are or where we're going.

Donald Trump, the temporary occupant of the White House, may lead a divided nation; or he may divide an already-fractured nation. If he can form a cohesive and compelling vision, he has a chance to do more than preside, he might actually be able to lead.

THE REFORM AGENDA

Our presidential campaigns are too long, too costly, too superficial, too personalized. In 2016, it gave us two candidates with high negatives who ran a scorched-earth campaign. In the end, we chose Trump.

What might we do to improve our presidential selection system?

- Somehow (overturning *Citizens United* and other Court decisions), we must reduce the role of big money in our political process.
- We should not allow each of our fifty states to have different election rules. We must pass national, uniform standards.
- We hold more elections than any other country. To increase interest and the importance of elections, we need to hold fewer elections.
- We should have voting on a three-day weekend, with Friday being National Election Celebration Day.
- We should directly elect our presidents and eliminate the Electoral College. If you were designing a constitutional republic from scratch, you would never invent an Electoral College. And in fact, no other nation has anything like it—for good reason. It is a relic of the past we should discard in favor of allowing the people to decide.

- We need to do something to make presidential debates more like genuine debates.

- We should not have Iowa (first caucus) and New Hampshire (first primary) to always start off our election cycles. These states are not representative of the nation as a whole, and we should rotate the two opening states in our elections.

- We should hold a series of regional primaries, not the mish mash we now have.

- We should open primaries to Independents (this might produce more moderate, less extreme candidates).

- We should rely more on Super-Delegates and less on activists to select our candidate.

- Reforming the primary system might also help. Some call for a national primary day, but a one-day winner-take-all would not allow for lesser-known candidates—like Obama, Sanders and Trump—to rise by winning primaries and caucuses and unseating the frontrunner.

- A better alternative might be to hold a series of 5–6 regional primaries[102], rotating which regions go first with each election. This would a) shorten the process; b) allow a lesser-known candidate to emerge; and c) be less costly.

OUR NATIONAL RORSCHACH TEST

What did the 2016 presidential race say about us, and what did it say about our country? Clearly this was not our finest election nor out finest hour. The 2016 race often seemed to bring out the worst in us. Neither candidate appealed to the good within us; neither candidate presented a hopeful, uplifting message. Both candidates got a great deal of mileage out of being harsh, critical, snarky, at times racist and misogynistic, and at times truly ugly. Trump's followers cheered when their candidate made openly racist statements,[103] and supported him even when he was exposed on the

Access Hollywood bus as someone who said about women: "Grab them by the p****. You can do anything."[104] They supported him when he openly mocked a handicapped news reporter,[105] mocked John McCain's military sacrifice,[106] attacked a Gold Star family,[107] claimed that an Indiana-born federal judge was biased because his parents came from Mexico,[108] called women a barrage of insulting names,[109] and the list goes on and on.

Clinton's supporters dismissed FBI accusations that she was careless in the way she handled classified materials. Her supporters were also dismissive of accusations of pay-for-play at the Clinton Foundation, unconcerned at her parsing of words relating to any and all criticisms, and not interested in her flip-flopping on issues such as TPP.

We can be this way because we think tribally. When someone in our tribe is attacked, we reflexively come to their defense. And we accept as fact, any charge leveled against members of the other tribe. We ascribe pure motives to our tribe, yet condemn the motives of the other tribe. Such toxic tribalism is why we defend Bill Clinton when charged with sexual indiscretions, but attack Donald Trump when faced with similar charges, and vice versa. We turn a blind eye to the sins of our tribe as we call for severe punishment when transgressions by the other tribe are made. Truth? Justice? They are drowned out by the deafening screams of tribal loyalties. This tribalism is evident in a political science department, a nation-state, and a political party. Us versus them. The good guys versus the bad guys. It makes life, and decision making so easy. And often, so wrong.

Tribalism is painfully obvious in the political wars that take place on a daily basis in Washington DC. We saw it in all its ugliness in late October when Senator John McCain said that Republicans intended to block any and all Supreme Court nominees should Hillary Clinton become president. A few days later he walked that comment back, but his original words accurately represented how political competition had morphed into all-out war. Is this any way to run a country?[110]

Do we force our leaders to be snarky, or do they lead us to that poisoned well? Perhaps this is a "chicken-or-egg" question. But could aspirational leadership rescue us from this morass? Or must the drive for civility in our public life be a grassroots movement that percolates up from the people to the politicians?

As a nation, we are all much the poorer for our descent into this dark place. It is not befitting a great nation. It calls into doubt our fitness to lead the world.

The greatest power that United States has is the example we set, the ideals towards which we reach, the justice we promote and the justness in our relations with others. When we live up to our highest ideals we stand out like a bright light in a dark and confusing world. Our best *is* good enough, if only we would be at our best.

Elections give us the opportunity not only to select leaders but also to conduct a national conversation about who we are, where we wish to go, how we hope to get there, and who will be at the helm during our journey.

They also give us a chance to exhibit our worst fears and impulses, our biases and hatred, our smallest and meanest selves. Know us by the direction in which we are moving. Know us by what we aspire to be, are willing to work for, choose to believe in. Know us by the quality of the people we elect, the soundness of our political beliefs, the size of our hearts, and the hand we extend in open friendship. It is our choice, our dream, and at times, our nightmare.

CONCLUSION TO THE CONCLUSION

Donald Trump is now our president. We should all wish him well because if he does well, American does well, and we do well. Being president is a thankless, impossible job.[111] The problems are big but the power to solve those problems is limited. Our system of separation of powers limits a president's power, and binds the president to a Congress that may be controlled by the political opposition.

The conditions that led to the rise of Donald Trump are real, and must be addressed. Globalization is having a profound impact on the United States, and we ignore its victims at our peril. As the editors of *The New Yorker* wrote:

> We are in the midst of a people's revolt, a great debate concerning income inequality, the "hollowing" of the middle, globalization's winners and losers. If the tribune whom the voters of the Republican Party have chosen is a false one, we cannot dismiss the message because we deplore the messenger. The white working-class voters who from the core of Trump's support—and who were once a Democratic constituency—should not have their anxieties and suffering written off. Their struggle with economic abandonment and an incomplete health-care system demands airing, under-standing, and political solutions.[112]

Elections have consequences. *Roe v. Wade* is in jeopardy. Obamacare is at risk. Immigration reform (as reform) may be dead. Trade deals are in jeopardy. Environmental reforms are in doubt. Taxes will go down. NATO may be less consequential. A "wall" may or may not be built.

And so, as writer and director Woody Allen said, "Before us are two paths. One leads to unimaginable suffering, anguish, and despair. The other to total extinction. Let us hope we have the wisdom to choose the right path."[113] Or, as the actress Bette Davis said, "Hang on boys, we're in for a bumpy ride."[114]

In the Senate, the Democrats picked up two seats (Illinois and New Hampshire), and picked up a few seats in the House, cutting into the Republican seat total lead, but failing to capture either House or Congress. Thus, the Republicans control the presidency, both Houses and Congress, and soon, a Supreme Court majority. What will they do with this power?

In 2016, the Republican voters came home, and the Democratic voters stayed home. Millennials, African Americans, Hispanics, all part of the Democratic/Obama coalition of 2008 and 2012 just did not bother to vote in sufficient numbers to bring about a Clinton victory.

Hillary Clinton just couldn't rally the Obama coalition that took him to victory in 2008 and 2012. It seems the Obama coalition was precisely that—the Obama coalition, and not the Democratic Party coalition.

President Donald J. Trump. Protest marches occurred in several major U.S. cities, transition planning was accelerated, allies needed to be reassured, adversaries needed to see a peaceful and seamless transition of power. The election was over and a new president was about to take the oath of office. Hope and fear.

New presidencies present us with reason to hope. This new president also gives us reason to pause, perhaps even to be worried. His promises were among the boldest ever delivered. In the first week following the election, he began backing off his promises: he probably wouldn't appoint a special prosecutor to indict, convict, and imprison Hillary Clinton;[115] he probably wouldn't round up and deport the 12 million undocumented people living in the U.S.;[116] he probably wouldn't ban all Muslims from entering the country;[117] and he would probably keep several key provisions of Obamacare.[118] But he probably would reverse U.S. approval of the Paris Climate agreement,[119] drop TPP,[120] maybe even pull out of the Iranian arms deal.[121]

Presidents are given too much credit when things go well, too much blame when things go wrong. Presidents are expected to solve all our problems, yet are not given the powers to accomplish that goal. Their power is too hot in some areas (foreign policy and war), too cold in other areas (domestic and economic policy), but unlike Goldilocks, we can't see to get it "just right."

We would do well as a country if we lowered our demands and expectations on presidents and government, heightened our vigilance over government activities, raised our level of awareness, enhanced our democratic involvement, and toned down our rhetoric as we raised our sense of community.

As the epicenter of the American political system, a tremendous amount of public and media attention is focused on the president. This creates the false impression that the president is the government. But in our system of checks and balances, power is fragmented. The presidency is but one of the three branches, and all presidents share power. And yet, because the president is the focus of so much of our attention we have come to expect—even demand —that the president solve our problems, even though they do not have the power to do so. Thus, when problems remain unsolved we blame the president. This expectation/ power gap contributes to our impression that the president is not up to the job, or has let us down.

In a democracy, people tend to get the government they deserve. For good or ill, we got Donald Trump; he is our president. And while the people chose Hillary Clinton (the popular vote winner), the Electoral College chose Trump, who is now the 45th president of the United States.

Notes

1. Dixie Liberal, "Remembering Adlai Stevenson," *Daily Kos*, July 14, 2009.
2. Liam Donovan, "The Blue Wall Crumbles," *National Review*, November 16, 2016.
3. "2016 Election Expert Polls," *The Washington Post*, November 29, 2016.
4. Alexander Agadjanian, "How the 2016 Vote Broke Down by Race, Gender, and Age," *Decision Desk HQ*, March 8, 2017.
5. Ibid.
6. Ibid.
7. Ibid.
8. Ibid.
9. Ibid.
10. Ibid.
11. Ibid.
12. Ibid.
13. Ibid.
14. *The Los Angeles Times*, "Why Trump Won," November 13, 2016, A1; See: Edison Research national exit poll. Regarding African American voters, see also https://www.washingtonpost.com/news/monkey-cage/wp/2016/11/11/trump-got-more-votes-from-people-of-color-than-romney-did-heres-the-data/?utm_term=.c32bb40bd497
15. Roper Center, "How Groups Voted in 2016," The Roper Center, April 24, 2017
16. Sarah Wheaton, "Van Jones: Trump Vote is a White-Lash," *POLITICO*, November 9, 2016.
17. Roper Center, "How Groups Voted in 2016."
18. Ibid.
19. Ibid.
20. Ibid.
21. Ibid.
22. Ibid.
23. Ibid.

24. George Packer, "The Unconnected," *The New Yorker*, October 31, 2016, 51

25. J.D. Vance, *Hillbilly Elegy: A Memoir of a Family and Culture in Crisis* (New York: HarperCollins, 2016).

26. See J.D. Vance, *Hillbilly Elegy*, New York: Harper, 2016.

27. Matthew Yglesias, "Why Did the South Turn Republican, *The Atlantic*, August 24, 2007.

28. James E. Campbell, "Forecasting the 2016 American National Election," *PS*, October 2016.

29. Peter W. Stevenson, "Trump is headed for a win, says professor who has predicted 30 years of presidential outcomes correctly," *The Washington Post*, September 23, 2016, https://www.washingtonpost. com/news/the-fix/wp/2016/09/23/trump-is-headed-for-a-win-says-professor-whos-predicted-30-years-of-presidential-outcomes-correctly/?utm_term=.9d920973e393.

30. See Theda Skocpol and Vanessa Williamson, *The Tea Party and the Remaking of Republican Conservatism* (New York: Oxford University Press, 2013).

31. Ibid.

32. Ibid.

33. Ibid.

34. Fareed Zakaria, "Where were Republicans Moderates 20 Years Ago?" *The Washington Post*, March 3, 2016, https://www.washingtonpost. com/opinions/where-were-republican-moderates-20-years-ago/20 16/03/03/4c1c49c2-e18b-11e5-846c-10191d1fc4ec_story.html

35. Quoted in David Frum, "The Rise of Populism," *The Week*, October 11, 2016, 5 .

36. Philip Bump, "Trump Got the Most GOP Votes Ever-Both For and Against Him," *The Washington Post*, June 8, 2016.

37. Dan Merica and Sophie Tatum, "Clinton expresses regret for saying 'half' of Trump supporters are 'deplorables'," CNN, September 12, 2016, http://www.cnn.com/2016/09/09/politics/hillary-clinton-donald-trump-basket-of-deplorables/.

38. Steve Phillips, "What About White Voters?" *Center for American Progress*, February 5, 2016.

39. Ibid.

40. Henry Enten, "Demographics Aren't Destiny," *Five Thirty Eight*, November 14, 2016.

41. "Compare U.S. Presidents," *Inside Gov*, http://us-presidents. insidegov.com

42. Ibid.

43. Jeremy Diamond, "Russian Hacking and the 2016 Election: What You Need to Know," *CNN*, December 16, 2016.

44. Ibid.

45. Ibid.

46. Ibid.

47. Ibid.

48. Ibid.

49. Reed Wilson, "Hacking the Election is Nearly Impossible – But that's not Russia's Goal," *The Hill*, September 16, 2016.

50. Kurt Eichenwald, "Why Vladimir Putin's Russia is Backing Donald Trump," *Newsweek Magazine*, November 4, 2016.

51. Glenn Harlan Reynolds, "'Crooked Hillary' Nickname Isn't Going Away," *USA Today*, September 26, 2016.

52. Liam Donovan, "The Blue Wall Crumbles," *National Review*, November 16, 2016.

53. Ibid.

54. Raymond Hogler, "What's Behind the Decline of Unions?" *New Republic*, November 30, 2016.

55. Ibid.

56. The American Presidency Project, "Presidential Elections Data," *University of California, Santa Barbara*, 2017.

57. Ibid.

58. Ibid.

59. Ibid.

60. See Matt Streb, Michael A. Genovese, et al, "Social Desirability and Support for a Female American President," *President Opinion Quarterly*, Spring 2008.

61. Editorial Board, "Republicans Attempt to Rig the Vote by Suppressing It," *The Washington Post*, November 7, 2016.

62. Elizabeth Kolbert, "Drawing the Line: How Redistricting Turned America from Blue to Red," *The New Yorker*, June 27, 2016.

63. Jasmine C. Lee, "How States Moved Toward Stricter Voter ID Laws," *The New York Times*, November 7, 2016, A12.

64. Ari Berman, "Blocking the Ballot Box," *The Los Angeles Times*, February 5, 2016, A15.

65. David Daley, *RATF**KED: The True Story Behind the Secret Plan to Steal America's Democracy*, Liveright, 2016.
66. *Washington Post*, November 7, 2016.
67. Theo Keith, "Former Republican staffer says GOP lawmakers were 'giddy; while crafting voter ID law," Fox6News, April 7, 2016, http://fox6now.com/2016/04/07/former-republican-staffer-says-gop-lawmakers-were-giddy-about-wisconsins-voter-id-law/.
68. Matt Gravatt, "Yelton was fired for saying what the NC GOP won't," *The Hill*, October 25, 2013.
69. Quoted from Michael Wines, "Some Republicans Acknowledge Leveraging State Voter ID Laws for Political Gain," *The New York Times*, September 20, 2016, A15.
70. Jonathan Burr, "Election 2016's Price Tag: 6.8 Billion," *CBS Money Watch*, November 8, 2016.
71. Ibid.
72. Niv Sultan, "Trump's Free Media," *Open Secrets*, April 13, 2017.
73. Gallup, "America's Trust in Mass Media Sinks to New Low," *Gallup Poll*, September 14, 2016.
74. Ibid.
75. David Frum, "No One is Doing More for Democratic Turnout than Donald Trump, *The Atlantic*, August 17, 2016.
76. Jessica Chasmar, "Donald Trump changed political parties at least five times: report," *The Washington Times*, June 16, 2015, http://www.washingtontimes.com/news/2015/jun/16/donald-trump-changed-political-parties-at-least-fi/.
77. Cathy Burke, "Clinton Won Richest Counties-64 percent of U.S. G.O.P," *Newsweek*, November 22, 2016.
78. Ibid.
79. Matthew Rozsa, "Omarosa Hints at a Donald Trump Enemies List," *SALON*, November 9, 2016; and Mary Bowerman, "Omarosa: Trump Already has an Enemies List," *USA Today*, November 8, 2016.
80. Andy Gilmore, "Truthliness," *The New York Times Magazine*, October 13, 2010.
81. Jonathan V. Last, "Dividers, Not Uniters," *Standard*, March 28, 2016.
82. Ibid.
83. Plato, *The Republic* (New York: Dover Thrift Editions, 2000).

84. See Dennis F. Thompson, "Constitutional Character: Virtues and Vices in Presidential Leadership," *Presidential Studies Quarterly*, March 2012, 23.

85. Celina Durgin, "The Definitive Roundup of Trump's Scandals and Business Failures," *National Review*, March 15, 2016, http://www.nationalreview.com/article/432826/donald-trumps-scandals-and-business-failures-roundup.

86. Editorial, "Donald Trump's List of Presidential Shortcomings Seems Bottomless. What Do We Do Now?" *The Los Angeles Times*, January 20, 2017.

87. Ibid.

88. Ibid.

89. Ibid.

90. Ibid.

91. Ibid.

92. Ibid.

93. Ibid.

94. Ibid.

95. Ibid.

96. Michael A. Genovese, Todd L. Belt, and William Lammers, *The Presidency and Domestic Policy* (Boulder: Paradigm Publishers, 2014).

97. Amy B. Wang, "Trump in 2012: 'The Electoral College is a Disaster for a Democracy," *The Washington Post*, November 9, 2016.

98. Brooke Singman, "Who's With Trump? Senate Republicans Deeply Split in Wake of Tape Controversy," Fox News, December 12, 2016.

99. Ibid.

100. Pew Research Center for the People and the Press, "Public Trust in Government: 1958–2014," www.people-press.org/2014/11/13/public-trust-in-government/.

101. David Plouffe, *The Audacity to Win: The Inside Story and Lessons of Barack Obama's Historic Victory* (New York: Viking, 2009).

102. See Larry Sabato, "America's Missing Constitutional Link," VQR, 2006.

103. Thomas Wood, "Racism Motivated Trump Supporters More than Authoritarianism," *The Washington Post*, April 17, 2017.

104. "p****" was vulgar slang for the female anatomy. See Jessica Taylor, "'You Can Do Anything': In 2005 Tape, Trump Brags About Groping, Kissing Women," NPR, October 7, 2016, http://

www.npr.org/2016/10/07/497087141/donald-trump-caught-on-tape-making-vulgar-remarks-about-women.

105. Editorial, "Why Donald Trump Should Not Be President," *The New York Times*, September 25, 2016.
106. Ibid.
107. Ibid.
108. Ibid.
109. Ibid.
110. See Nathaniel Persily, ed., *Solutions to Political Polarization in America* (Cambridge University Pres, 2015).
111. Thomas E. Cronin, Michael A. Genovese, and Meena Bose, *The Paradoxes of the American Presidency*, 5th edition (New York: Oxford University Press, 2017).
112. The Editors, "Talk of the Town," *The New Yorker*, October 31, 2016, 32–33.
113. See Woody Allen Quotes, *Goodreads*, 2016.
114. Adapted from *All About Eve*, 20th Century Fox, 1950.
115. Daniella Diaz, "Trump on 'Lock Her Up' Chant: 'Now We Don't Care,'" *CNN*, December 10, 2016.
116. BBC Reports, "Trump's Promises Before and After the Election," *BBC*, June 1, 2017.
117. Ibid.
118. Ibid.
119. Ibid.
120. Ibid.
121. Ibid.

POSTSCRIPT

THE AFTERMATH

As if the election itself wasn't enough, in the weeks following the Trump upset victory, what was merely an election-time blip—the alleged role Russia may have played in the election—exploded into a front-page story.

As inauguration day approached, the case of Russian interference in the presidential election heated up. All seventeen U.S. intelligence agencies confirmed what they had long suspected and warned about, that the Russian government, under orders from Vladimir Putin, hacked into the computer systems of key Democrats—including Clinton's campaign chairman John Podesta—stole information, gave the stolen information to Julian Assange's WikiLeaks, who released the materials. This proved damaging to the Clinton campaign and may have impacted the outcome of the election.[1]

Donald Trump refused to accept this, arguing that he was not convinced that the Russians were involved, going so far as to dismiss the allegations as a "witch hunt."[2] Trump siding with Vladimir Putin and Julian Assange[3] against what would soon become his own intelligence services put the new President Trump at odds not only with the Democrats in Congress (which might be expected), but also against many leading Republican legislators such as Senators John McCain and Lindsey Graham (not to mention the seventeen U.S. intelligence agencies). Trump, sensitive to the possibility that this might tarnish his electoral victory, simply refused to believe the voluminous evidence and chose to believe what he wanted— perhaps "needed"—to believe.

Late in the afternoon of Friday, January 7, a partially declassified Intelligence Report on the Russian hacking was released. It was a devastating indictment of Vladimir Putin and Russia. The report confirmed that Russia carried out a comprehensive cyber campaign designed to hurt Hillary Clinton and help elect Donald Trump as president. This cyber campaign was ordered by Vladimir Putin who "aspired to help" elect Trump.[4]

Also on Friday afternoon, president-elect Trump sat for one of his infrequent security briefings where the evidence of the Russian cyberattack was presented to him. After the meeting, Trump insisted that the cyber campaign had no impact on his victory, but he did seem to entertain the possibility that there might have been some sort of cyberattack.[5]

THE POSTELECTION VERDICT

Russian Meddling: The Old Cold War Heats Up

Russia, under the direction of Vladimir Putin, interfered with the 2016 U.S. presidential election[6] intending to hurt Hillary Clinton and help Donald Trump.[7] Did this have an impact on the election? It is hard to say. Clearly the continual drip-drip-drip releases of WikiLeaks stories that were supplied to them by the Russians put Hillary Clinton on the defensive in the final weeks of the campaign, and these stories played into Donald Trump's narrative in his attacks against Clinton, but how many voters were swayed by this?

President-elect Trump and his surrogates went to great lengths to dismiss questions, and even ridicule the reports of Russian tampering in an U.S. election, but the accumulated evidence told a different story.[8] The Russians got what they wanted: the defeat of Hillary Clinton, and the election of Donald Trump. But did their intrusion into the process *cause* the result?

Both Republican and Democratic lawmakers demanded an investigation. Trump tried to deflect these efforts.[9]

THE ELECTORAL COLLEGE DECIDER

Although Hillary Clinton won the popular (democratic) vote by roughly 2.9 million, the people don't actually elect the president, the Electoral College does. Winning *states*, not *votes*, is what matters.[10]

When the presidency was invented almost 230 years ago, the Framers were perplexed regarding just who should select the new president. Should it be Congress? No, that would undermine the separation-of-powers model that was designed to prevent executive tyranny. The people? No, a skilled president could inflame the passions of the people and turn them into a mob at his disposal, or conversely, the people might demand that the president bend to their will, and that could mean the president would be a slave to the whim of the moment. After much deliberation and frustration, they ended up inventing an Electoral College, wherein each state would select a slate of electors from among the finest in local society, and they would choose the president. No other country in the world has such a bizarre system, and for good reason.

This Electoral College opens the door to two potential problems: 1) the winner of the popular vote might not win the electoral vote

(2000 and 2016), or 2) between the time of the election and the actual voting and counting of the Electoral College votes, some form of mischief might occur.

There are 538 Electors comprising the Electoral College. On December 19, in their respective state capitol, they meet to cast their electoral votes, presumably for the candidate to whom they are pledged, and who won in the state. Theses votes are the transmitted to the Congress where on the opening of the new Congress, the results are read out and the election is official. That five-week period between the November 8 vote, and the December 19 electoral vote has been a time of intense if hidden lobbying by the losers designed to sway votes away from the presumptive winner.

Ordinarily, the electors are loyal to the candidate to whom they are pledged, but over our history there have been several "faithless electors" who ended up voting for someone else. Is that permitted? Several states prescribe legal penalty to electors who are faithless, and over twenty states require a party loyalty pledge of their electors, but apply no real punishment if they defect. So, most electors are in effect free agents whose vote might be bought or otherwise gained.

In 2004, 30 percent of the electors said they had been contacted about switching their votes, and in 2012, 80 percent, according to Robert Alexander of Ohio Northern University, an expert on the Electoral College and presidential electors,[11] said they were lobbied to switch candidates. If the past is prelude, we should not be surprised if similar and even more intense lobbying took place in this election.

On several occasions in our history, the candidate who lost the popular vote has won the presidency, but never has an Electoral College vote actually overturned the presumptive winner of a presidential election. And while it is unlikely to be successful this year, the seeds of mischief can produce some bitter fruit. The delegitimation of a president, as was attempted unsuccessfully in the "birther" movement so persistently used by Donald Trump against President Obama, could once again hamstring or even detail the newly elected president as he or she tried to govern our divided nation. We've had enough division and hatred. We need some governing.

In the end, the Electoral College rebellion against Trump did not materialize. And while there were faithless electors, more of them turned against Hillary Clinton (5) than against Trump. He won the Electoral College 304-227.

The U.S. has had three consecutive two-term presidencies, Bill Clinton, George W. Bush, and Barack Obama were popular enough to each get reelected, so why the backlash? In those twenty-four years, the U.S. economy grew from $9.5 trillion to over $16 trillion in real terms.[12] The digital revolution was American led. There were no wars between major powers for over seventy years, and the United States remained the only true superpower in the world. Cause for celebration? So what went wrong?

Globalization and the fears and displacement it generated? Hyper change? Wage stagnation? Job insecurity? The rise of "the other" (having an African American president and almost having a female president)? Middle America snubbing the likes of Davos / Ted Talks elites? The sense that the world was spinning out of control and our presidents were helpless in the face of these changes.

Did the U.S. vote merely for a change of party, or for a change of regime? The popular rage that carried Trump into office was both a rejection of the status quo and an embrace of a wholly new way of governing. Liberal Democracy projected weakness; Trump's illiberal democracy would project strength.

Did Trump sow the anger abroad in the land, or merely channel and exploit it? As *The Economist* noted, "his voters took Mr. Trump seriously but not literally, even as his critics took him literally but not seriously."[13]

White voters without a college degree made up a third of the electorate, and voted for Trump over Clinton by 39 points![14] But disappointment, even angry white voters are one thing; Trump also attracted—as he spoke for—a hateful, dangerous, sexist, white supremacist fringe of voters bent on spreading hatred and racial tension.

PRESIDENT TRUMP

On January 20, 2017, Donald J. Trump took the oath of office. His inaugural address was dark and divisive—just like his campaign.[15] There was no pivot, no mellowing, no new Trump, no presidential Trump, no call for unity, no "bring-us-together" theme. He intended to govern as he campaigned.

For the second time in a decade, the winning candidate lost. That is, the candidate who won the popular vote lost in the Electoral College and was therefore denied the presidency. Vice President Al Gore won the popular vote by over half a million votes (48.4% to 47.9%) yet lost to George W. Bush in the Electoral College by a slim 271-266 margin. In 2016, Secretary Hillary Clinton beat Donald Trump by nearly 3 million votes (48% to 45.9%) yet lost in the Electoral College by a 306-232 margin. Not very democratic, but that is the system that the Framers invented.

Every four years, we get to pick one person to "serve us" as President of the United Sates. Sometimes we pick a good one, sometimes not. Sometimes the choice is between two strong candidates, often not. In 2016, voters were highly disappointed with both candidates. Did we end up with the lesser of two evils, or the evil of two lessers, or will Donald Trump surprise the establishment that he

so often attacked and become a great president? Whether liberal
or conservative, Democrat or Republican, left or right, it is in all
our interests to have our presidents succeed. When the president
succeeds, we the nation succeeds.

NOTES

1. Brian Bennett and Noah Bierman, "Trump Renews Attack on Case for Russian Hacking," *The Los Angeles Times*, January 5, 2017, A1
2. Mark Landler, "Trump, Citing 'a Witch Hunt,' Denies Any Collusion with Russians," *The New York Times*, May 18, 2017.
3. Ibid.
4. Greg Miller, "Declassified Report Says Putin 'Ordered' Effort to Undermine Faith in U.S. Election and Help Trump," *The Washington Post*, January 6, 2017.
5. Ibid.
6. Eric Liptor, David E. Sanger and Scott Shane, "The Perfect Weapon: How Republican Cyberpower Invaded the U.S.," *The New York Times*, December 13, 2006.
7. Adam Entous and Ellen Nakashima, "FBI in Agreement with CIA that Russia Aimed to Help Trump Win White House," *The Washington Post*, December 16, 2016
8. Erin Kelly and Eliza Collins, "The Republican Congress is Quickly Becoming Trump's Biggest Problem," *USA Today*, May 17, 2017.
9. Ibid.
10. In the three key rust belt states that Trump won, he won Michigan by about 10,200 votes, Wisconsin by 22,175 votes, and Pennsylvania by 70,600 votes. Less than 100,000 voters swayed the election to Trump.
11. See Robert Alexander, *Presidential Electors and the Electoral College* (Amherst, NY: Cambria Press, 2012).
12. Mark J. Perry, "Putting the Ridiculously Large $18 Trillion U.S. Economy into Perspective," *AEI Ideas*, June 10, 2015.
13. *The Economist*, "The Trump Era," November 12, 2016, 9.
14. Nate Cohn, "Why Trump Won: Working-Class Whites," *The New York Times*, November 9, 2016.
15. Politico Staff, "Full Text: Donald Trump Inauguration Speech Transcript," *POLITICO*, January 20, 2017.

APPENDIX

TRUMP'S CONVENTION
ACCEPTANCE SPEECH

The following is a transcript of Donald Trump's address to the
Republican National Convention*:

> Friends, delegates and fellow Americans: I humbly and grate-
> fully accept your nomination for the presidency of the United
> States.
>
> Together, we will lead our party back to the White House,
> and we will lead our country back to safety, prosperity, and
> peace. We will be a country of generosity and warmth. But
> we will also be a country of law and order.
>
> Our Convention occurs at a moment of crisis for our nation.
> The attacks on our police, and the terrorism in our cities,
> threaten our very way of life. Any politician who does not
> grasp this danger is not fit to lead our country.
>
> Americans watching this address tonight have seen the
> recent images of violence in our streets and the chaos in our

communities. Many have witnessed this violence personally, some have even been its victims.

I have a message for all of you: the crime and violence that today afflicts our nation will soon come to an end. Beginning on January 20th 2017, safety will be restored.

The most basic duty of government is to defend the lives of its own citizens. Any government that fails to do so is a government unworthy to lead.

It is finally time for a straightforward assessment of the state of our nation.

I will present the facts plainly and honestly. We cannot afford to be so politically correct anymore.

So if you want to hear the corporate spin, the carefully-crafted lies, and the media myths the Democrats are holding their convention next week.

But here, at our convention, there will be no lies. We will honor the American people with the truth, and nothing else.

These are the facts:

Decades of progress made in bringing down crime are now being reversed by this Administration's rollback of criminal enforcement.

Homicides last year increased by 17% in America's fifty largest cities. That's the largest increase in 25 years. In our nation's capital, killings have risen by 50 percent. They are up nearly 60% in nearby Baltimore.

In the President's hometown of Chicago, more than 2,000 have been the victims of shootings this year alone. And more than 3,600 have been killed in the Chicago area since he took office.

The number of police officers killed in the line of duty has risen by almost 50% compared to this point last year. Nearly 180,000 illegal immigrants with criminal records, ordered deported from our country, are tonight roaming free to threaten peaceful citizens.

The number of new illegal immigrant families who have crossed the border so far this year already exceeds the entire total from 2015. They are being released by the tens of thousands into our communities with no regard for the impact on public safety or resources.

One such border-crosser was released and made his way to Nebraska. There, he ended the life of an innocent young girl named Sarah Root. She was 21 years-old, and was killed the day after graduating from college with a 4.0 Grade Point Average. Her killer was then released a second time, and he is now a fugitive from the law.

I've met Sarah's beautiful family. But to this Administration, their amazing daughter was just one more American life that wasn't worth protecting. One more child to sacrifice on the altar of open borders. What about our economy?

Again, I will tell you the plain facts that have been edited out of your nightly news and your morning newspaper: Nearly Four in 10 African American children are living in poverty, while 58% of African American youth are not employed. 2 million more Latinos are in poverty today than when the President took his oath of office less than eight years ago. Another 14 million people have left the workforce entirely.

Household incomes are down more than $4,000 since the year 2000. Our manufacturing trade deficit has reached an all-time high—nearly $800 billion in a single year. The budget is no better.

President Obama has doubled our national debt to more than $19 trillion, and growing. Yet, what do we have to show for it? Our roads and bridges are falling apart, our airports are in Third World condition, and forty-three million Americans are on food stamps.

Now let us consider the state of affairs abroad.

Not only have our citizens endured domestic disaster, but they have lived through one international humiliation after another. We all remember the images of our sailors being forced to their knees by their Iranian captors at gunpoint.

This was just prior to the signing of the Iran deal, which gave back to Iran $150 billion and gave us nothing—it will go down in history as one of the worst deals ever made. Another humiliation came when president Obama drew a red line in Syria—and the whole world knew it meant nothing.

In Libya, our consulate—the symbol of American prestige around the globe—was brought down in flames. America is far less safe—and the world is far less stable—than when Obama made the decision to put Hillary Clinton in charge of America's foreign policy.

I am certain it is a decision he truly regrets. Her bad instincts and her bad judgment—something pointed out by Bernie Sanders—are what caused the disasters unfolding today.

Let's review the record. In 2009, pre-Hillary, ISIS was not even on the map.

Libya was cooperating. Egypt was peaceful. Iraq was seeing a reduction in violence. Iran was being choked by sanctions. Syria was under control. After four years of Hillary Clinton, what do we have? ISIS has spread across the region, and the world. Libya is in ruins, and our Ambassador and his staff were left helpless to die at the hands of savage killers. Egypt was turned over to the radical Muslim brotherhood, forcing the military to retake control. Iraq is in chaos.

Iran is on the path to nuclear weapons. Syria is engulfed in a civil war and a refugee crisis that now threatens the West. After fifteen years of wars in the Middle East, after trillions of dollars spent and thousands of lives lost, the situation is worse than it has ever been before.

This is the legacy of Hillary Clinton: death, destruction and weakness.

But Hillary Clinton's legacy does not have to be America's legacy. The problems we face now—poverty and violence at home, war and destruction abroad—will last only as long as we continue relying on the same politicians who created them. A change in leadership is required to change these outcomes. Tonight, I will share with you my plan of action for America.

The most important difference between our plan and that of our opponents, is that our plan will put America First. Americanism, not globalism, will be our credo. As long as we are led by politicians who will not put America First, then we can be assured that other nations will not treat America with respect. This will all change in 2017.

The American People will come first once again. My plan will begin with safety at home—which means safe neighborhoods, secure borders, and protection from terrorism. There can be no prosperity without law and order. On the economy, I will outline reforms to add millions of new jobs and trillions in new wealth that can be used to rebuild America.

A number of these reforms that I will outline tonight will be opposed by some of our nation's most powerful special interests. That is because these interests have rigged our political and economic system for their exclusive benefit.

Big business, elite media and major donors are lining up behind the campaign of my opponent because they know she will keep our rigged system in place. They are throwing money at her because they have total control over everything she does. She is their puppet, and they pull the strings.

That is why Hillary Clinton's message is that things will never change. My message is that things have to change— and they have to change right now. Every day I wake up determined to deliver for the people I have met all across this nation that have been neglected, ignored, and abandoned.

I have visited the laid-off factory workers, and the communities crushed by our horrible and unfair trade deals. These are the forgotten men and women of our country. People who work hard but no longer have a voice.

I AM YOUR VOICE.

I have embraced crying mothers who have lost their children because our politicians put their personal agendas before the national good. I have no patience for injustice, no tolerance for government incompetence, no sympathy for leaders who fail their citizens.

When innocent people suffer, because our political system lacks the will, or the courage, or the basic decency to enforce our laws—or worse still, has sold out to some corporate lobbyist for cash—I am not able to look the other way.

And when a Secretary of State illegally stores her emails on a private server, deletes 33,000 of them so the authorities can't see her crime, puts our country at risk, lies about it in every different form and faces no consequence—I know that corruption has reached a level like never before.

When the FBI Director says that the Secretary of State was "extremely careless" and "negligent," in handling our classified secrets, I also know that these terms are minor compared to what she actually did. They were just used to save her from facing justice for her terrible crimes.

In fact, her single greatest accomplishment may be committing such an egregious crime and getting away with it—especially when others have paid so dearly. When that same Secretary of State rakes in millions of dollars trading access and favors to special interests and foreign powers I know the time for action has come.

I have joined the political arena so that the powerful can no longer beat up on people that cannot defend themselves. Nobody knows the system better than me, which is why I alone can fix it. I have seen firsthand how the system is rigged against our citizens, just like it was rigged against Bernie Sanders—he never had a chance.

But his supporters will join our movement, because we will fix his biggest issue: trade. Millions of Democrats will join our movement because we are going to fix the system so it works for all Americans. In this cause, I am proud to have at my side the next Vice President of the United States: Governor Mike Pence of Indiana.

We will bring the same economic success to America that Mike brought to Indiana. He is a man of character and accomplishment. He is the right man for the job. The first task for our new Administration will be to liberate our citizens from the crime and terrorism and lawlessness that threatens their communities.

America was shocked to its core when our police officers in Dallas were brutally executed. In the days after Dallas, we have seen continued threats and violence against our law enforcement officials. Law officers have been shot or killed in recent days in Georgia, Missouri, Wisconsin, Kansas, Michigan and Tennessee.

On Sunday, more police were gunned down in Baton Rouge, Louisiana. Three were killed, and four were badly injured. An attack on law enforcement is an attack on all Americans. I have a message to every last person threatening the peace on our streets and the safety of our police: when I take the oath of office next year, I will restore law and order our country.

I will work with, and appoint, the best prosecutors and law enforcement officials in the country to get the job done. In this race for the White House, I am the Law And Order candidate. The irresponsible rhetoric of our President, who has used the pulpit of the presidency to divide us by race and color, has made America a more dangerous environment for everyone.

This Administration has failed America's inner cities. It's failed them on education. It's failed them on jobs. It's failed them on crime. It's failed them at every level.

When I am President, I will work to ensure that all of our kids are treated equally, and protected equally.

Every action I take, I will ask myself: does this make life better for young Americans in Baltimore, Chicago, Detroit, Ferguson who have as much of a right to live out their dreams as any other child America?

To make life safe in America, we must also address the growing threats we face from outside America: we are going to defeat the barbarians of ISIS. Once again, France is the victim of brutal Islamic terrorism.

Men, women and children viciously mowed down. Lives ruined. Families ripped apart. A nation in mourning.

The damage and devastation that can be inflicted by Islamic radicals has been over and over—at the World Trade Center, at an office party in San Bernardino, at the Boston Marathon, and a military recruiting center in Chattanooga, Tennessee.

Only weeks ago, in Orlando, Florida, 49 wonderful Americans were savagely murdered by an Islamic terrorist. This time, the terrorist targeted our LGBT community. As your President, I will do everything in my power to protect our LGBT citizens from the violence and oppression of a hateful foreign ideology. To protect us from terrorism, we need to focus on three things.

We must have the best intelligence gathering operation in the world. We must abandon the failed policy of nation building and regime change that Hillary Clinton pushed in Iraq, Libya, Egypt and Syria. Instead, we must work with all of our allies who share our goal of destroying ISIS and stamping out Islamic terror.

This includes working with our greatest ally in the region, the State of Israel. Lastly, we must immediately suspend immigration from any nation that has been compromised by terrorism until such time as proven vetting mechanisms have been put in place.

My opponent has called for a radical 550% increase in Syrian refugees on top of existing massive refugee flows coming into our country under President Obama. She proposes this despite the fact that there's no way to screen these refugees in order to find out who they are or where they come from. I only want to admit individuals into our country who will support our values and love our people.

Anyone who endorses violence, hatred or oppression is not welcome in our country and never will be.

Decades of record immigration have produced lower wages and higher unemployment for our citizens, especially for African American and Latino workers. We are going to have an immigration system that works, but one that works for the American people.

On Monday, we heard from three parents whose children were killed by illegal immigrants Mary Ann Mendoza, Sabine Durden, and Jamiel Shaw. They are just three brave representatives of many thousands. Of all my travels in this country, nothing has affected me more deeply than the time I have spent with the mothers and fathers who have lost their children to violence spilling across our border.

These families have no special interests to represent them. There are no demonstrators to protest on their behalf. My opponent will never meet with them, or share in their pain. Instead, my opponent wants Sanctuary Cities. But where was sanctuary for Kate Steinle? Where was Sanctuary for the children of Mary Ann, Sabine and Jamiel? Where was sanctuary for all the other Americans who have been so brutally murdered, and who have suffered so horribly?

These wounded American families have been alone. But they are alone no longer.

Tonight, this candidate and this whole nation stand in their corner to support them, to send them our love, and to pledge in their honor that we will save countless more families from suffering the same awful fate.

We are going to build a great border wall to stop illegal immigration, to stop the gangs and the violence, and to stop the drugs from pouring into our communities. I have been honored to receive the endorsement of America's Border

Patrol Agents, and will work directly with them to protect the integrity of our lawful immigration system.

By ending catch-and-release on the border, we will stop the cycle of human smuggling and violence. Illegal border crossings will go down. Peace will be restored. By enforcing the rules for the millions who overstay their visas, our laws will finally receive the respect they deserve.

Tonight, I want every American whose demands for immigration security have been denied—and every politician who has denied them—to listen very closely to the words I am about to say.

On January 21st of 2017, the day after I take the oath of office, Americans will finally wake up in a country where the laws of the United States are enforced. We are going to be considerate and compassionate to everyone.

But my greatest compassion will be for our own struggling citizens. My plan is the exact opposite of the radical and dangerous immigration policy of Hillary Clinton. Americans want relief from uncontrolled immigration. Communities want relief.

Yet Hillary Clinton is proposing mass amnesty, mass immigration, and mass lawlessness. Her plan will overwhelm your schools and hospitals, further reduce your jobs and wages, and make it harder for recent immigrants to escape from poverty.

I have a different vision for our workers. It begins with a new, fair trade policy that protects our jobs and stands up to countries that cheat. It's been a signature message of my campaign from day one, and it will be a signature feature of my presidency from the moment I take the oath of office.

I have made billions of dollars in business making deals—
now I'm going to make our country rich again. I am going to
turn our bad trade agreements into great ones. America has
lost nearly-one third of its manufacturing jobs since 1997,
following the enactment of disastrous trade deals supported
by Bill and Hillary Clinton.

Remember, it was Bill Clinton who signed NAFTA, one of
the worst economic deals ever made by our country.

Never again.

I am going to bring our jobs back to Ohio and to America—
and I am not going to let companies move to other countries,
firing their employees along the way, without consequences.

My opponent, on the other hand, has supported virtually
every trade agreement that has been destroying our middle
class. She supported NAFTA, and she supported China's
entrance into the World Trade Organization—another one
of her husband's colossal mistakes.

She supported the job killing trade deal with South Korea. She
has supported the Trans-Pacific Partnership. The TPP will
not only destroy our manufacturing, but it will make America
subject to the rulings of foreign governments. I pledge to
never sign any trade agreement that hurts our workers, or
that diminishes our freedom and independence. Instead, I
will make individual deals with individual countries.

No longer will we enter into these massive deals, with many
countries, that are thousands of pages long—and which no
one from our country even reads or understands. We are
going to enforce all trade violations, including through the
use of taxes and tariffs, against any country that cheats.

This includes stopping China's outrageous theft of intellectual
property, along with their illegal product dumping, and

their devastating currency manipulation. Our horrible trade agreements with China and many others, will be totally renegotiated. That includes renegotiating NAFTA to get a much better deal for America—and we'll walk away if we don't get the deal that we want. We are going to start building and making things again.

Next comes the reform of our tax laws, regulations and energy rules. While Hillary Clinton plans a massive tax increase, I have proposed the largest tax reduction of any candidate who has declared for the presidential race this year—Democrat or Republican. Middle-income Americans will experience profound relief, and taxes will be simplified for everyone.

America is one of the highest-taxed nations in the world. Reducing taxes will cause new companies and new jobs to come roaring back into our country. Then we are going to deal with the issue of regulation, one of the greatest job-killers of them all. Excessive regulation is costing our country as much as $2 trillion a year, and we will end it. We are going to lift the restrictions on the production of American energy. This will produce more than $20 trillion in job creating economic activity over the next four decades.

My opponent, on the other hand, wants to put the great miners and steel workers of our country out of work—that will never happen when I am President. With these new economic policies, trillions of dollars will start flowing into our country.

This new wealth will improve the quality of life for all Americans—We will build the roads, highways, bridges, tunnels, airports, and the railways of tomorrow. This, in turn, will create millions more jobs. We will rescue kids from failing schools by helping their parents send them to a safe school of their choice.

My opponent would rather protect education bureaucrats than serve American children. We will repeal and replace disastrous Obamacare. You will be able to choose your own doctor again. And we will fix TSA at the airports! We will completely rebuild our depleted military, and the countries that we protect, at a massive loss, will be asked to pay their fair share.

We will take care of our great Veterans like they have never been taken care of before. My opponent dismissed the VA scandal as being not widespread—one more sign of how out of touch she really is. We are going to ask every Department Head in government to provide a list of wasteful spending projects that we can eliminate in my first 100 days. The politicians have talked about it, I'm going to do it. We are also going to appoint justices to the United States Supreme Court who will uphold our laws and our Constitution.

The replacement for Justice Scalia will be a person of similar views and principles. This will be one of the most important issues decided by this election. My opponent wants to essentially abolish the 2nd amendment. I, on the other hand, received the early and strong endorsement of the National Rifle Association and will protect the right of all Americans to keep their families safe.

At this moment, I would like to thank the evangelical community who have been so good to me and so supportive. You have so much to contribute to our politics, yet our laws prevent you from speaking your minds from your own pulpits.

An amendment, pushed by Lyndon Johnson, many years ago, threatens religious institutions with a loss of their tax-exempt status if they openly advocate their political views.

I am going to work very hard to repeal that language and protect free speech for all Americans. We can accomplish these great things, and so much else—all we need to do is start believing in ourselves and in our country again. It is time to show the whole world that America Is Back—bigger, and better and stronger than ever before.

In this journey, I'm so lucky to have at my side my wife Melania and my wonderful children, Don, Ivanka, Eric, Tiffany, and Barron: you will always be my greatest source of pride and joy. My Dad, Fred Trump, was the smartest and hardest working man I ever knew. I wonder sometimes what he'd say if he were here to see this tonight.

It's because of him that I learned, from my youngest age, to respect the dignity of work and the dignity of working people. He was a guy most comfortable in the company of bricklayers, carpenters, and electricians and I have a lot of that in me also. Then there's my mother, Mary. She was strong, but also warm and fair-minded. She was a truly great mother. She was also one of the most honest and charitable people I have ever known, and a great judge of character.

To my sisters Mary Anne and Elizabeth, my brother Robert and my late brother Fred, I will always give you my love you are most special to me. I have loved my life in business.

But now, my sole and exclusive mission is to go to work for our country—to go to work for all of you. It's time to deliver a victory for the American people. But to do that, we must break free from the petty politics of the past.

America is a nation of believers, dreamers, and strivers that is being led by a group of censors, critics, and cynics.

Remember: all of the people telling you that you can't have the country you want, are the same people telling you that I wouldn't be standing here tonight. No longer can we rely on those elites in media, and politics, who will say anything to keep a rigged system in place.

Instead, we must choose to Believe In America. History is watching us now.

It's waiting to see if we will rise to the occasion, and if we will show the whole world that America is still free and independent and strong.

My opponent asks her supporters to recite a three-word loyalty pledge. It reads: "I'm With Her". I choose to recite a different pledge.

My pledge reads: "I'M WITH YOU—THE AMERICAN PEOPLE."

I am your voice.

So to every parent who dreams for their child, and every child who dreams for their future, I say these words to you tonight: I'm With You, and I will fight for you, and I will win for you.

To all Americans tonight, in all our cities and towns, I make this promise: We Will Make

America Strong Again.

We Will Make America Proud Again.

We Will Make America Safe Again.

And We Will Make America Great Again.

THANK YOU.

* "Full text: Donald Trump's 2016 RNC draft speech transcript," *POLITICO*, July 21, 2016.

Figure 2. Donald Trump acceptance speech to the Republican National Convention in Cleveland, Ohio. July 21, 2016.

Source. Voice of America, https://commons.wikimedia.org/wiki/File:Donald_Trump_2016_RNC_speech_(4).jpg.

Figure 3. Bernie Sanders & Hillary Clinton. July 12, 2016.

Source. Photo by Marc Nozell, https://commons.wikimedia.org/wiki/
File:Bernie_Sanders_%26_Hillary_Clinton_(28205920271).jpg.

Figure 4. Michelle Obama speaks at a Hillary Clinton presidential campaign rally at Southern New Hampshire University. October 13, 2016.

Source. Photo by Tim Pierce, https://commons.wikimedia.org/wiki/File:Michelle_Obama_at_SNHU_October_2016.jpg.

Figure 5. U.S. Senator Tim Kaine at a campaign rally at the Maryvale Community Center in Phoenix, Arizona. November 3, 2016.

Source. Photo by Gage Skidmore, https://commons.wikimedia.org/wiki/File:Tim_Kaine_(30749030226).jpg.

Figure 6. Governor Mike Pence at a at an immigration policy speech hosted by Donald Trump at the Phoenix Convention Center in Phoenix, Arizona. August 31, 2016.

Source. Photo by Gage Skidmore, https://commons.wikimedia.org/ wiki/Category:Mike_Pence_vice_presidential_campaign,_2016#/media/ File:Mike_Pence_(28757100633).jpg.

Figure 7. President Donald Trump being sworn in at the U.S. Capitol building in Washington, D.C. January 20, 2017.

Source. White House Photo, https://commons.wikimedia.org/wiki/ File:Donald_Trump_swearing_in_ceremony.jpg.

Figure 8. President Donald J. Trump, Mr. Barack Obama and their wives, Mrs. Melania Trump and Michelle Obama, stand on the East steps of the U.S. Capitol during the 58th Presidential Inauguration, Washington D.C. January 20, 2017.

Source. Photo by Air Force Staff Sgt. Sean Martin, https://commons. wikimedia.org/wiki/File:Donald_Trump,Barack_Obama,_Melania_ Trump,_Michelle Obama_at_U.S._Capitol_01-20-17.jpg.

INDEX

PRAISE FOR *THE TRUMPING*
OF AMERICAN POLITICS

"Anyone who wants to understand the unique and often bizarre 2016 presidential election needs to read this book by Michael A. Genovese. This timely, well-researched, hard-hitting, and comprehensive account of the 2016 primaries and general election should be read by scholars, students, and the general public."

—James Thurber, American University

* * * * *

"What happened in 2016? How could Clinton lose and Trump triumph? Ingenious political scientist Michael A. Genovese explains that enough working class whites were captivated by Trump's television celebrity status and by his attitude: anti-politics, anti-Washington, anti-incumbent, etc...Still, it is a complicated and puzzling story. Genovese makes sense of it and proposes provocative reforms in this tight, highly readable treatise."

—Thomas E. Cronin, Colorado College

* * * * *

"One of the nation's most astute and prolific scholars of the presidency walks the reader through the tumultuous and unprecedented 2016 elections with wit, skill, and clarity, elucidating key moments, but also the larger lessons and principles that frame his analysis. An accessible and insightful book."

—Robert Spitzer, SUNY Cortland

* * * * *

"In this book, Michael Genovese carefully walks us through the details of the 2016 election and its immediate aftermath. This is a valuable, indeed essential undertaking. Genovese's book performs the indispensable task of specifically documenting why Trump challenges and threatens democratic norms. This is not a partisan rant, but a clear-eyed assessment that describes what went wrong in 2016, why the U.S. presidential election process in general is deeply flawed and how it can be fixed."

—Chris Edelson, American University

* * * * *

"Michael Genovese's book, *The Trumping of American Politics*, is an engaging, entertaining, comprehensive examination of one of the most controversial presidential elections in U.S. history. Once readers start on the book, they will surely want to finish it."

—Matthew Streb, Northern Illinois University